The Novel

D1638396

The Literary Agenda

The Novel

A Survival Skill

TIM PARKS

OXFORD
UNIVERSITY PRESS

OXFORD

UNIVERSITY PRESS

Great Clarendon Street, Oxford, OX2 6DP,
United Kingdom

Oxford University Press is a department of the University of Oxford.
It furthers the University's objective of excellence in research, scholarship,
and education by publishing worldwide. Oxford is a registered trade mark of
Oxford University Press in the UK and in certain other countries

© Tim Parks 2015

The moral rights of the author have been asserted

First Edition published in 2015

Impression: 3

Published in the United States of America by Oxford University Press
198 Madison Avenue, New York, NY 10016, United States of America

British Library Cataloguing in Publication Data
Data available

Library of Congress Control Number: 2015936769

ISBN 978–0–19–873959–3

Printed in Great Britain by
Clays Ltd, St Ives plc

Series Introduction to the Literary Agenda

The Crisis in, the Threat to, the Plight of the Humanities: enter these phrases in Google's search engine and there are 23 million results, in a great fifty-year-long cry of distress, outrage, fear, and melancholy. Grant, even, that every single anxiety and complaint in that catalogue of woe is fully justified—the lack of public support for the arts, the cutbacks in government funding for the humanities, the imminent transformation of a literary and verbal culture by visual/virtual/digital media, the decline of reading . . . And still, though it were all true, and just because it might be, there would remain the problem of the response itself. Too often there's recourse to the shrill moan of offended piety or a defeatist withdrawal into professionalism.

The Literary Agenda is a series of short polemical monographs that believes there is a great deal that needs to be said about the state of literary education inside schools and universities and more fundamentally about the importance of literature and of reading in the wider world. The category of "the literary" has always been contentious. What *is* clear, however, is how increasingly it is dismissed or is unrecognized as a way of thinking or an arena for thought. It is sceptically challenged from within, for example, by the sometimes rival claims of cultural history, contextualized explanation, or media studies. It is shaken from without by even greater pressures: by economic exigency and the severe social attitudes that can follow from it; by technological change that may leave the traditional forms of serious human communication looking merely antiquated. For just these reasons this is the right time for renewal, to start reinvigorated work into the meaning and value of literary reading for the sake of the future.

It is certainly no time to retreat within institutional walls. For all the academic resistance to "instrumentalism," to governmental measurements of public impact and practical utility, literature exists in and across society. The "literary" is not pure or specialized or self-confined; it is not restricted to the practitioner in writing or the academic in studying. It exists in the whole range of the world which is its subject-matter: it consists in what non-writers actively receive from writings when, for example, they start to see the world more imaginatively as a result of reading novels and begin to think more carefully about human personality. It comes from literature making available much of human life that would not otherwise be existent to thought or recognizable as knowledge. If it is true that involvement in literature, so far from being a minority aesthetic, represents a significant contribution to the life of human thought, then that idea has to be argued at the public level without succumbing to a hollow rhetoric or bowing to a reductive world-view. Hence the effort of this series to take its place *between* literature and the world. The double-sided commitment to occupying that place and establishing its reality is the only "agenda" here, without further prescription as to what should then be thought or done within it.

What is at stake is not simply some defensive or apologetic "justification" in the abstract. The case as to why literature matters in the world not only has to be argued conceptually and strongly tested by thought, it should be given presence, performed and brought to life in the way that literature itself does. That is why this series includes the writers themselves, the novelists and poets, in order to try to close the gap between the thinking of the artists and the thinking of those who read and study them. It is why it also involves other kinds of thinkers—the philosopher, the theologian, the psychologist, the neuro-scientist—examining the role of literature within their own life's work and thought, and the effect of that work, in turn, upon literary thinking. This series admits and encourages personal voices in an unpredictable variety of individual approach and expression, speaking wherever possible across countries and disciplines and temperaments. It aims for something more than intellectual assent: rather the literary sense of what it is like to feel the thought, to embody an idea in a person, to bring it to being in a narrative or in aid of adventurous reflection. If the artists refer to their own works, if other thinkers return to ideas that have marked much of their working life, that is not their vanity nor a failure of originality. It is what the series has asked of them: to speak out of what they know and care about, in whatever language can best serve their most serious thinking, and without the necessity of trying to cover every issue or meet every objection in each volume.

Philip Davis

Foreword

Let me invite the reader to put aside, for the space of this book, all received ideas about the nature and uses of literature in general and narrative fiction in particular. Let me beg you, for example, to renounce the idea that fiction is undeniably a good thing, a liberal thing, a life-enhancing thing, that the act of writing, and of reading, is of its nature intrinsically positive and always and assiduously to be encouraged. Let me ask you in particular to relinquish the notion that a literary author is unquestionably "on the right side" in some struggle of civilization against barbarism, good against evil, or that he or she is necessarily wise or demonstrably more perceptive or receptive than the average person, and so on and so forth.

You might also want to suspend any belief that human beings require a constant supply of stories to make sense of the world, and that this need is met by literature, by fiction, which hence becomes an essential part of the mental food chain and thus urgently to be defended against all foes. Finally, why not try to imagine that there is no justifiable self esteem to be attached to the mere writing and reading of novels, however literary or sophisticated, or brilliantly entertaining they may be, nor any ultimate "need" for their existence, simply an appetite on the part of many for their consumption and a willingness on the part of the few to satisfy that appetite.

Is this too hard? Perhaps you find it impossible to put aside, however briefly, the convictions of a lifetime, convictions shared and repeatedly reinforced by literature teachers, critics, academics, and indeed all right-thinking people. But if, despite an honourable effort, you just cannot accept the idea that literature might be as much part of the problem as the solution, at least the attempt will have given you a fresh awareness of the powerful positive qualities we attach to authorship; hence you will be alerted to one important aspect of writerly ambition and consequently of the writer/reader relationship.

To write and publish and "become an author" is to assume a privileged position in society and to place yourself on the winning side of an unassailable hierarchy: the writer always trumps the reader.

However young and inexperienced, the published author will be interviewed and indeed looked upon as someone with special and important knowledge about the human condition. Over time, as he or she explores and grows into the role society grants to the artist, embraces or rejects the opportunity to play the moralist, or alternatively the rebel—but the two so often coincide—to be constantly visible, or to retreat into a provocative invisibility; or again as his established authorship alters the dynamic in his marriage, his family, his circle of friends, allowing him perhaps to live in a four-star hotel (Joyce), to acquire a little cottage in the country (Beckett), or a private plane (Faulkner), it is impossible that this role he has assumed, this way of living—for writing and publishing is the author's *life*—not be reflected in the way he writes, the way he addresses the reader, in the characters who appear in his writing and the stories they are involved in. In turn, each individual reader's attitude to the status of writing and the position of the writer—the writer he is reading at the moment and writers in general—will affect his or her response to what he reads, strengthen resistance or encourage greater sympathy. For where there is hierarchy, at least in an era of individualism, there is inevitably tension and suspicion, competition even, but also adulation and reverence; the latter, after all, are reassuring emotions, we like to feel them, and then there are so few people before whom one can bow down these days without losing a little face.

This brief study presents itself not as "literary criticism"—or certainly not in the way that term is usually understood—but an account, at once psychological, anthropological perhaps, or sometimes simply narrative, of the role writing assumes in different authors' lives—what did it mean for Dickens to write and publish a novel, what did it mean for Chekhov, how did it fit in with social background and family, with the pattern of relationships the author had formed before publication and would form afterwards? Above all, I want to suggest how inevitably this is reflected in the writing itself; that there is, as it were, a continuity of atmosphere between everything that writing means for the writer and everything that happens in his writing. Quite simply, whether we're talking about Beckett or Thomas Hardy, D. H. Lawrence or J. M. Coetzee, the writing and publication of a novel is an event in the author's life, and a moment of communication, not just, and perhaps not even primarily, with the public, but also with those close to the author; an event that moves their lives on perhaps, or perhaps allows some chronic paralysis to persist.

The novel, then, is not some magically separate art object entire unto itself, but something plucked from the flow of a life. The reader encounters the author through what he has written and a relationship is established, one that will be not entirely distinct from the kind of relationships the author seeks in his life, or that readers form in theirs. Rather than dissecting a text by close reading, or rather, in *addition* to dissecting the text, I will be talking about encounters between writer and reader, meetings, acquaintances, friendships, that may be positive or perhaps extremely negative, depending where each of the parties is coming from. These are meetings that can be abruptly aborted, after a few pages perhaps, or endlessly repeated, even if dissatisfying, even if we can't understand why we come back for more pain, or more banality. The business of books and reading is so much more precarious, fluctuating, fleeting, and complex than our rather exclusive tradition of literary criticism would have us believe.

And where am *I* coming from, you will ask? It's a fair question, and I will try to say something about this in Chapter 4. I will try to say a little about the kind of event a novel can be in my life, whether a novel I have written or a novel I am reading. I shall not say too much to avoid embarrassment, which already tells you more than is wise (but "wisdom" will not get us very far). In particular, though, I hope the reader will begin to compare the pattern of what I like and dislike (or am indifferent to) with the pattern of what he likes and dislikes, or couldn't care less about. I don't want you to be persuaded or drawn to my position on the authors we talk about, only to suggest that your position, like mine, is not due to a recognition of any absolute quality in the author, but the result of a meshing or failure to mesh between two people with two different visions of the world, which might be complementary or could be contradictory. As for me, your literary likes and dislikes are part of the wider pattern of your relationships, and not unconnected with the kind of family you have, the kind of life you lead.

So although writing in general, *tout court*, may not necessarily be "good," or even "a good thing," it can be a very lively thing; I mean it's part of the business of living. When we open a novel, as with any encounter, we move into an area of risk.

Acknowledgement

This book relies heavily on thinking coming out of the field of systemic psychology and in particular on the writing of the distinguished Italian psychologist Valeria Ugazio. I make no apologies for that. Close friends for a decade or more, Valeria and I discuss each other's work regularly; our conversations have been among the most stimulating of my life. It is a great pleasure to acknowledge my debt to her here.

Contents

Contents

1
Four Imagined Meetings

Imagine we meet James Joyce, Jim, in the flesh. We're on the seafront in Trieste shortly before the Great War, on Kreuzstrasse in Zurich in 1918, on the Boulevard Saint Michel in the thirties.

What do we talk about?

There's a script that many attested to.[1]

First of all a few names are mentioned, people we know in common perhaps. Irish people of course. Dubliners that is. We speak about Dublin. We're not in Dublin, but Dublin is always the main point of reference, for Joyce. If you know someone, a Dubliner, who has said something about Joyce, so much the better. Whether flattering or critical hardly matters. What's important is that they were talking about Joyce, in Dublin. We might then mention the author's most recent publication, praising it. He will want to know if we have understood some subtlety, some fine point that might have escaped us. Indeed it has. He's pleased. He starts to explain. It's rather a long explanation, taking in Vico, St Thomas Aquinas. He knows so much more than you do. But he wears his learning lightly.

The opening courtesies over, Joyce asks you to run a little errand for him. He is carrying a heavy envelope. Perhaps a manuscript. Alas, our long talk means he no longer has time to take it to the Post Office. Could you do that for him? Or could you take a message to his brother, Stanislaus? Or to Svevo? Or to Shakespeare & Company, the Paris bookshop that is publishing *Ulysses*?

If you say yes, the next time you meet he will have another errand for you, something more time-consuming perhaps.

If you say yes again, the next time you meet he will ask you if you might lend him a few pounds, a few liras, a few francs. A few hundred francs. The script does not change with the years. Joyce will never arrive at a point where he is so well off as not to ask an admirer for a loan. Whether he is living, as he often did live, in a four-star hotel, or in a miserable garret, he will ask for a loan.

If you grant him a loan, the next time you meet he may well ask for another. Bigger. Meantime he hasn't paid back the previous loans. But you never expected him to. Instead he tells you about a recent holiday, with the family: his wife Nora, his son Giorgio, his daughter Lucia, maybe a sister or two. He has a strong sense of family. If you stop in a café for tea, or a beer, or five beers, or a whisky or three, he will leave the waiter a huge tip. He's a very nice guy.

But first you have to talk about the urgent matter of his next literary effort. Are you willing to spend some time discussing *Ulysses*, or his Work in Progress? That is, to listen to Jim discussing his Work in Progress? Yes? Let's go then.

If there is a political crisis in the air, or even a war, something you can't get out of your mind, Joyce will say: Oh, but let's leave the Czechs/Poles/Slavs in peace, and talk about my Work in Progress.

It's natural that if you're writing something yourself, you might want to give it to him to read, to reciprocate as it were. Don't worry when it doesn't get mentioned again. If he hasn't bothered reading Pound's *Cantos* yet, when Pound is doing so much for him, he's hardly likely to read yours. Just accept that this relationship is one-way traffic.

Later Jim will ask you an even bigger favour. Can you read to him, in the afternoons, for an hour perhaps? He has problems with his eyes. He's not seeing too well. Can you correct some proofs for him? Or maybe take down some dictation? Or type up a manuscript?

Why do you agree to do all these onerous favours? Because Joyce is a genius. Everyone says so. He has told you himself. And when you read his books you feel he really is. You feel it even more when he reads his work out loud to you in his musical Irish voice. He loves reading to people. He is charismatic. You have the impression that Joyce is your meeting with history. It's an honour to help the man.

And of course you're not alone. Everybody's helping him. Famous people too. "He is *formidable*," said Philippe Soupault. "You go to see him; he asks which way you will be going when you leave. You say, 'To the Étoile,' and before you know it he has you doing an errand for him at the Bastille."[2] "If God almighty came down to earth," Nora would say to James "you'd have a job for him."[3]

Who are you to hang back?

Yet the day comes when it all seems too much. The demands he's making on your time and your wallet are too insistent. And sometimes the requests seem stupid. "He got people . . . to follow him wherever he wanted . . ." remarked one of the most assiduous helpers, Stuart Gilbert, "to [cancel] their arrangements if he wanted their assistance for some trivial, easily postponed task . . ." (Bowker, 385). It's exhausting. And while at the beginning the little difficulties and mild offences of *Dubliners* were exciting and the greater challenges of *A Portrait* mind expanding, and *Ulysses* despite all the obscenity and abstruseness simply monumental, nevertheless you're now finding the first chapters of Work in Progress beyond you, bewildering.

> What clashes here of wills gen wonts, oystrygods gaggin fishygods! Brékkek Kékkek Kékkek Kékkek! Kóax Kóax Kóax! Ualu Ualu Ualu! Quaouauh! Where the Baddelaries partisans are still out to mathmaster Malachus Micgranes and the Verdons catapelting the camibalistics out of the Whoyteboyce of Hoodie Head. Assiegates and boomeringstroms. Sod's brood, be me fear! Sanglorians, save![4]

What is all this about? you wonder. When will I ever have time to decipher it?

So inevitably the day comes when you find yourself saying no to Joyce.

Could you go to the post office on Rue de . . .

No.

You never loved me, Joyce says. You never really cared.

And it's over. The great writer doesn't want to have anything more to do with you. You have betrayed him, the same way thousands of readers will betray him when the great man asks too much of them, when they just feel they can't go on. Even the closest relatives and friends eventually "betrayed" him. Even Stanislaus, even Pound. It's understandable. The question rather is, why do some hang on to the bitter end? Who are these people who read *Finnegans Wake* right through and would give Joyce the shirt off their backs? And why did he need to demand that of us?

Charles Dickens will not ask us to lend him money, though he may complain about how much money *he* is lending or simply giving to children, parents, relatives, friends, and even people he hardly knows at all. Despite all the complaints, it's quite possible that if we seem needy enough or *worthy* enough, he will offer us money, or work, without our having to ask him.

How might one meet the great man? In a train, perhaps, for he is an indefatigable traveller, to and from his book readings, his visits to his mistress, his trips to Europe. A 12-year-old American girl met him on a train in 1868, totally charmed him, was totally charmed by him, and managed to write a vivid account about the meeting forty-four years later, so intense was the memory.[5] But vivid accounts of meeting Dickens are legion. He loved to turn on the charm. He loved the *theatre* of meetings, the act of seduction. Each novel opening had to be absolutely enticing.

Cemeteries, hospitals, prisons, are other places we might run into the novelist; he never fails on his travels to stop and explore the worlds of those who have been, as it were, excluded from life, in one way or another, as he was once excluded as a little boy, sent out to work in a miserable factory while his sister continued to frequent a prestigious music college. Or we might meet him at one of the many clubs he is member of: the Garrick or the Reform, though in this case we would have to be an insider as much as he was. Not everyone can walk into the Garrick; you have to be invited. For Dickens, writing novels is a way of getting into those hallowed places. He simply *loves* clubs; wasn't his first novel about a club, in the end? The Pickwick Club.

If you are a young lady and have been a bad girl you might meet Dickens in Shepherds Bush, where he interviews applicants for admission to a Home for Homeless Women. Homeless is a euphemism for prostitute. Even in these cases it is perfectly possible to charm Dickens and be charmed by him, though that isn't always enough. To get into the home, and stay in it, you have to convince him and keep convincing him of your *worthiness*. He is not beyond expelling a favourite inmate from the home if she doesn't observe the tough rules, laid down by himself. Ultimately, if you manage to stay on the right side of the writer/philanthropist for a couple of years, this particular conversation will lead to a ticket for Australia where, like Little Em'ly from *David Copperfield*, you can start life again with your stained character washed clean in ten thousand miles of salty ocean.

In happier circumstances, Dickens meets us with expansiveness. He entertains. It's unlikely he'll be alone when you meet him. There is a dinner party, at a club or his home. You are, so to speak, a spectator in the audience. Perhaps you have been invited to one of his famous Twelfth Night celebrations, with much merriment and theatricals. Dickens eats and drinks heartily and will be glad if you do so too. He is dressed colourfully, a green jacket perhaps, or red, frilly shirts, diamond studs. They are the clothes of someone who expects to be at the centre of attention. He launches into mimicry; of people and types whom everyone knows. He's hilarious and it's great fun to watch him do this. Sit back, let your glass be filled and enjoy the great man's performance, clap and cheer. But don't even think of emulating him. Dickens is, by his own devising, "the Inimitable One,"[6] "his own God as Trollope unkindly put it" (Tomalin, *Dickens*, Cast List). At most he might get his children to perform, or to, as it were, *reflect* his own performance. The twelfth night of Christmas is his eldest's birthday. So long as they are still youngsters and there is no real competition, it's amusing to have plenty of children around aping their more important elders.

If he likes you Dickens will invite you to further hearty meals and performances. If you are a struggling writer, he may take you under his wing. Dickens actually reads other people's manuscripts and may even publish them in the magazine he runs, *Household Words*. Every page of the magazine has the name Charles Dickens at the top, but it will never have your name, because the articles themselves are always anonymous. To publish in *Household Words* is to enter a club. The Dickens club. Behind Charles Dickens march a host of others, friends, acquaintances, business associates, characters, and caricatures. An Us. You are welcome to join, if you are worthy.

If, after one or two meetings, Dickens feels you have a bit of character to you, he may invent a nickname for you. He loves being the one who decides what people are called. And if you become a really good friend and are already famous in your own right, he may dedicate a novel to you. He may even name one of his children after you. There are ten children and they all have at least two names, plus fifteen novels all with dedicatees, so it is not such a long shot.

If Dickens feels able to confide in you, you will be asked to join him on one of his so-called "jaunts," by which he means an epic walk, perhaps right across London, perhaps in the dead of night. On these occasions the gloomy side of Dickens may emerge. He has spent so much energy entertaining people who perhaps didn't really deserve entertaining. Now, he wants to form a world apart, of just the two of you. A superior world. Are you up to it?

Befriending Dickens will not be without its trials. If, for example, you have better things to do when he wants to go on a jaunt, he will not take it kindly. If, God forbid, you should marry someone he doesn't approve of, that could be a major problem. Later, when Dickens leaves his wife, banishes her from the family, because this mother of ten children is now, in his estimation, lazy, uncaring, unworthy, you must take his side *unreservedly*, otherwise your friendship is over.

To be Dickens's friend in this later period of his life is rather trickier than it used to be. There is a secret we all know: Dickens has a mistress, nearly thirty years younger than himself, an actress. We can't mention her because for him to admit to this relationship would be to risk seeming unworthy himself of the vast family of respectable friends and readers he has spent a lifetime putting together.

This will be the sadness of our conversation with Dickens. It started so well, so warmly, it was so *memorable*, but where can we go with it now, especially if to keep impressing and entertaining us he has to deny himself the domestic happiness he loves to present as life's main goal? In his mid fifties Dickens stops writing for periods to concentrate on giving large public readings. On stage he loves to play both the very evil characters and the very good, winding up the comedy and melodrama to an extraordinary degree. By the end the audience is going quite wild. Then the great man hurries off in the dark to catch a train to wherever he has hidden his mistress.

How long can this go on? Dickens is so obviously overdoing it that you are hardly surprised when the great man collapses and dies, at 58, overwhelmed with the effort of being at the centre of attention so long, beside a partner who must never be seen.

But if we feel bereft at his passing, because Dickens really was so amusing, so memorable, so seductive, we can always join the Dickens Fellowship. Or the Dickens Pickwick Club. There are branches throughout the world. We can get together with other friends, other readers to remember how charmed we were, how overwhelmed by his brilliant and benevolent mimicry. It is usually the early books we talk about. The first meeting. We are the community of Dickens lovers.

You will not write a vivid account of your first meeting with Thomas Hardy. Perhaps you are at a country church service in Dorset. Hardy doesn't believe in God but never misses church. Perhaps you are at a grand funeral in London. Hardy never misses a funeral either, if he can help it. Either way you will have to look hard to find him in the congregation, or among the mourners. His clothes are nondescript, even his features seem slightly blurred, as if worn or eroded, as if he might simply fade into the crowd, or the landscape.

When you are introduced, he will ask kindly after your health, as if genuinely concerned. He is also concerned that you may be planning to write about the encounter, so it would be wise to indicate that you have no such ambitions. Tell him that your family has old Dorset connections and he will perk up. An uncle who was a schoolmaster in Weymouth perhaps, a great-grandfather buried in Puddletown. Unassuming, he will not impose himself on the conversation. Behind his bald head his hair is thin and long. He seems shy, modest, letting others do the talking, frowning at his wife's endless wittering, perhaps saying a sharp word to her. You have the impression he is kind to everyone but his wife, yet needs her the way he needs the church that he doesn't believe in. Now she is talking about the death of their faithful old dog, now about a bicycle ride to Winterbourne, now about an aristocratic neighbour. Hardy sends her a scornful glance. Then smiles at you. On political matters he will make only one or two demurring remarks. He will not declare himself. Perhaps he doesn't trust you. He wants to hear what you think first. When he says something about not believing in God it is done in such a way that you hardly notice, as if there were no implications. You are just beginning to think there is something more interesting and mysterious about him when it's time to part.

If you are invited to a second meeting with Hardy, perhaps at his home, Max Gate, which he designed himself, in the Dorset countryside, you are struck by the ugly squatness of the house, carefully hidden behind tall thick hedges, by the stodginess of the food, by the quietness of your host. Not that he doesn't cheer up sometimes, but often it's as if he'd found a way both to be there and not to be there; he's in a different dimension. His hand extended in greeting is a little limp, a little damp, not quite like a real hand. Anyway, he doesn't like to be touched. So you begin to notice the servants, the maids. There's a very cute young maid serving at table. And a cute young cousin. It's hard to focus on Thomas Hardy with these fleshy young people around, though it's clear the author is aware of them. Very aware. In fact there seems to be a relation between their intense presence and his almost absence. The wife fills all the gaps in the conversation. She is talking about the colours of the Italian countryside, then about her own literary efforts. It makes Hardy a little nervous.

If you are an academic or from an academic community he may be more forthcoming. He may talk about geology or evolution or determinism. He's well informed, in the way someone who reads all the recent publications is well informed. He may ask you about your cloistered world, with a note of envy in his voice. Perhaps he's angling for an invitation. You realize that the protection of academe might have spared him his wife.

Only if you are a young woman might this meeting with Hardy lead to something. He may write a note asking to meet again. If you are ambitious and write fiction yourself he may agree to recommend a short story of yours to a friendly publisher. He may even offer to help you improve it. In that case it will definitely be published. How generous of him! When he comes to London he'll agree to meet you in a museum, or to visit a cathedral. He's very bright and bushy-tailed now, very knowledgeable about the architecture. Above the droopy moustache and under the bald dome, his eyes are full of longing. Beneath a gargoyle, he makes a declaration of love. He loves you with all his heart. But somehow he manages to do it in such an inconsequential way that it's easy to protest your innocence, protest your marriage vows, or simply put things off. It's as if it's happening but it isn't happening. He doesn't move to touch you. He doesn't try to kiss you. Even before you've said no, he seems disappointed, but relieved.

Afterwards, you have the distinct impression that he wanted you to refuse. An embrace would have been too dangerous. He's married and prominent. Society would condemn him. Dimly, and for the first time, you connect this mild-mannered, modest, withdrawing man with the terrifying world of *Tess of the D'Urbervilles* and *Jude the Obscure*, books that had you weeping and wishing you'd never started them, but so beautiful. Now he sends you a brief poem in which a sudden change of weather intervenes to prevent a couple from becoming lovers.[7] They don't make a second attempt. The last time you see him he points out a baby hedgehog half eaten by hawks. When you talk to a close friend about him you say how polite he always was, how he aroused but also froze a certain desire to protect him.

D. H. Lawrence has no problem touching. Thin and wiry though he is, he is not in danger of fading into the crowd or the landscape. The hair is red, the beard vigorous, the movements likewise. Frequently ill, he won't ask for assistance. If he wants a loan, it's because he needs it and will pay it back. You may meet him in Sicily, in Ceylon, in Australia, in America, but wherever it is, meeting Lawrence means meeting Frieda too, and you can't really know Lawrence without knowing Frieda. They too like to meet couples rather than singles. They like to compare relationships.

When you and your partner arrive, he's busy. He's scrubbing the floors on his hands and knees. He's making furniture. Or he's sitting under a tree writing (quickly) in an exercise book with a pencil, occasional throwing stones at a lizard. Immediately, he confronts you. He invites you in. Frieda is preparing the dinner, or she is playing the piano. Lawrence begins to express loud opinions, criticizing whatever country you're in. He hates it. It's so decadent. His voice is squeaky. He loves it. The people are so authentic. He loves hating it. He has to leave. He's glad he came. If you express an opinion, he tells you you are wrong, you should change your opinion to his. He's right about this. He gives you a string of examples. He's persuasive. Probably he *is* right.

A festive feeling of conflict is in the air. Frieda hits a wrong note on the piano and Lawrence yells at her. She rounds on him. She won't be bullied. She stands up. She's so much more bulky and solid than he is. But he runs at her. Or he throws a dish at her. Or a knife. There are other guests and you're all rather shocked but then surprisingly everything has calmed down and he is singing along while she plays piano and it's as if the argument never happened. Your relationship should be more candid and alive, he tells you. Like ours. You're too buttoned up. You can't express yourselves.

Lawrence never hesitates to tell you what he thinks. He cracks a good joke and laughs and fondles the dog, then slaps it when it growls. But Frieda has spoiled the chicken and they are yelling at each other again. Lawrence isn't well. His breathing is hard. But maybe it's because he's not well that he feels free to be so bloody-minded, as if his illness was a kind of anger. Anyway Frieda gives as good as she gets. If only he would stop getting in her way in the kitchen, the food would be fine, she tells him. There's a broken plate on the floor.

Would you like to join us in a spiritual community? Lawrence asks when finally you're chewing the food, which actually isn't that bad in the end. For a while he harangues you. This ideal community will be on a remote island. Or in Florida perhaps. It will be made up of just a few men and women both honourable and fearless. The problem with all our modern relationships is that society doesn't provide the proper context for men and women to form authentic sex relations with each other. We must have the courage to break out.

It does sound like an interesting project, you tell him, but what about, er, practicality? Where, when, how? Lawrence is irritated. If you don't want to come it's because you're scared, because you've always needed your mother to do all your laundry, he says. Frieda says not to let him bully you and there they are shouting at each other again. I am not afraid of seeming ridiculous! he screams. No doubting him there.

Later when he takes the dog out he invites you to come with him. He is looking for a man to form a close friendship with, he says, a special friendship. A *Blutbrüderschaft*. He stops. Bats! See. Disgusting creatures! There are bats wheeling through the tree branches in the twilight. Fantastic! What he means is an intense friendship with another man at once so intimate and so open that both can say *exactly* what they think of each other without the friendship being put at risk. Complete freedom within an indissoluble bond tied by the mixing of blood.

As he says this, he puts a hand on your wrist, looking up for the bats again. It's a strong hand and he's so seductive you are almost afraid. You just know you mustn't say yes. But you're tempted to overcome that fear. You stall. It's the response he's expecting. Where's that damn dog, he shouts. Bloody hell! He starts to call the dog. You rascal! You scallywag! I'll thrash the living daylights out of you, if you don't come home this instant.

When you and your partner leave towards midnight you feel absolutely exhausted, as if you'd spent all evening locked into a wrestling match. We should write about them, you say, they're incredible. I bet he's already writing about us, your wife observes.

Too bad his will be the better book.

Notes

1. Every detail in this chapter is taken in one way or another from biographies of the four authors' lives.
2. Gordon Bowker, *James Joyce: A Biography* (New York: Farrar, Straus and Giroux, 2012), 385. Hereafter cited as "Bowker."
3. Richard Ellmann, *James Joyce* (Oxford University Press, 1982), 699. Hereafter cited as "Ellmann."
4. James Joyce, *Finnegans Wake* (Oxford World Classics, 2012), 4. Hereafter cited as "*Finnegans.*"
5. Kate Douglas Wiggin met Dickens on a train in 1868 and published her account in 1912.
6. Claire Tomalin, *Charles Dickens, A Life* (London: Viking, 2011), Prologue. Hereafter cited as "Tomalin, *Dickens.*"
7. "A Thunderstorm in Town," in *Thomas Hardy, The Complete Poems*, ed. James Gibson (London: Palgrave, 2001), 312. Hereafter cited as "*Hardy Poems.*"

2

Schismogenesis and Semantic Polarities

The previous chapter offered sketches, fragments of testimonies woven together, maliciously perhaps, mere provocations you could object. All the same you can see what I'm suggesting: that there is a continuity, in terms of tone, the kinds of emotions generated, the kinds of stories and relationships that can occur, between the life and the work. Not, crudely, that the work narrates events in the life, but that it is absolutely in line with the author's whole being, the things he does, the way he behaves, indeed *the work is a part of his behaviour*, so that a meeting with the author has analogies with an immersion in the text. One is introduced to the same world of thought and emotion.

I have occasionally had the good fortune to observe this in the flesh. I shall never forget my first meeting with J. M. Coetzee when it seemed at once and uncannily, from the tone of his voice, his body language, from a strange play between austerity and warmth, between withdrawal and openness, that I was actually *in* one of his narratives. Not that I was seeing Coetzee as one of the protagonists of his books or myself as involved in a Coetzee plot; it was the emotional tone of the whole encounter, a tone in which I, first as reader of his books and now as person meeting Coetzee, was playing as much a part as Coetzee himself; the tone was the fizz of *my* meeting *him*. Central to this tone, or feeling, was an apprehension of difficulty, the same I have always felt in the opening pages of any novel of Coetzee's: am I, or am I not going to let myself be put off by his apparent coldness, which I somehow sense is *merely* apparent? There is a curious double gesture of seduction (competence, charm, mystery) and aloofness (disregard, coldness, dismissal) in Coetzee's manner that was exactly the same in the flesh as on the page; or at least I felt that. So that just as when reading Coetzee I always have to decide whether I have the patience to proceed, similarly on meeting him I had to decide whether it was worth waiting for this frostiness to thaw.

It was after this meeting, happily followed by three or four others, that it occurred to me that the genius of Coetzee was to have found a way to create in words and narrative precisely and overwhelmingly the very unusual aura that he himself emanates, to have allowed us to come into his uneasy company through the books. Indeed, I would like readers to consider this as a possible description of creativity: the ability to produce, in a convention like narrative fiction—but it could be a painting, or a piece of music—the emotional tone and the play of forces in which the narrator lives, the particular mental world in which he moves. Far from being something one can take for granted, communication of this kind requires extraordinary authenticity and precision. Throughout the twentieth century, as the practice of literary criticism developed, there was much talk of the virtues of eliminating the personality of the author from the work. Yet when we return now to the writers who were presumed to have achieved this— Eliot and Joyce and Beckett—we find their work drenched with their personalities, supreme expressions of their manner and character and behaviour, each absolutely recognizable, triumphantly unmistakable, thanks to their creative powers. Try to talk about this, however, in academic circles and you are immediately accused of "biographical fallacy." Here is a definition:

> Biographical fallacy: the belief that one can explicate the meaning of a work of literature by asserting that it is really about events in its author's life. Biographical critics retreat from the work of literature into the author's biography to try to find events or persons or places which appear similar to features of the work, and then claim the work "represents those events, persons, or places," an over-simplified guess about Neo-formalist "mimesis." New Criticism considers it "fallacious" (illogical) because it does not allow for the fact that poets use their imaginations when composing, and can create things that never were or even things that never could be.[1]

Certainly one can agree that there is nothing more banal than saying that a book is "about" events in the author's life, then concentrating our attention on those events rather than on the book, though it may often be interesting to consider events in the author's life beside similar events in his or her novels precisely to savour the transformation that has occurred. Certainly I hope that in this book, once I have established my argument, we will focus on each writer's work with a renewed sense of how it relates to us, precisely through understanding its complex relation to the author's life. In general, though, this definition is rather more naive than the "fallacy" it seeks to dismiss; for inevitably when a poet uses his imagination to create things "that never were or even things that never could be," this creation comes out of his life in some way—how could it be otherwise?—and then becomes an event in his life, an integral part of the biography.

Imagination works on material that is available. Then, like it or not, when an author tells a story, even if set in some fantasy world, it will be *assumed* he is talking about, or alluding to the society he lives in, and quite possibly the people he knows. And the way that society and those people are talked about, or *believe* they are being talked about, will establish, perhaps transform, the author's relation to them. Again, this is a biographical fact. Once it has happened an author cannot not be aware of this connection and will react accordingly. Publication of books as different as *The Pickwick Papers*, *Ulysses*, *The Rainbow*, *Mrs Dalloway*, *The Satanic Verses*, are life events, in that they radically alter the vision others have of the writer and how he or she stands in relation to the world described in the books. Dickens is immediately loved as one who appears to love the world of the reader, he is an admirable compatriot, almost a personal friend. Joyce is immediately considered both a genius, superior to the reader, and a purveyor of obscenity, a threat to social well-being. Lawrence is reckoned a traitor to his country, evil and possibly mad. Woolf overtakes her husband in income and celebrity, an important turning point in any marriage. Salman Rushdie receives a death sentence.

These developments potentially condition the way the next work is written, depending on how the author reacts to the public's reaction to his or her work; life is all about reaction and anticipating the reaction of others. Authors very quickly become aware that their writings have personal implications. Then there are the spouses. Aside from the alteration in their partner's status, it would be hard for the wives or husbands of authors not to feel, as they read a novel that presents, say, marriages and love affairs, that their relationship is not somehow touched by what is told there, perhaps altered, perhaps redefined. Or at least, this is something the author knows he risks when he writes a work that narrates a marriage. Hardy's first wife was furious about much of the material in *Tess of the D'Urbervilles* and *Jude the Obscure*. Hardy's second wife was furious about the poems he wrote in memory of the first. Hardy no doubt foresaw those reactions, yet wrote the works just the same, or wrote them in part to elicit those reactions. Certainly the two wives believed he had foreseen their reactions, and this sense that he had foreseen them increased their indignation, which again was something he would probably have foreseen. And so on. To the point that one wonders whether this wasn't actually Hardy's way of communicating with those around him, since all accounts suggest that he found more direct methods of communication extremely difficult.

It's not unthinkable, then, that the tension in a writer's work might have much to do with his or her perception of how those close to him will respond to what he is writing. It's true that the novel is officially addressed to everyone—it is published, made public—but there might also be a way in which it can be thought of as a communication *overheard*. Or rather, once I become aware that this novel was *also* inevitably a communication between the author and those close to him how can I exclude that knowledge from my reading of the book, and the way I react to it? When I read Dostoevsky's *Notes from the Underground*, where the anonymous narrator foresees for the prostitute how she will die of tuberculosis in the brothel, humiliated in every way, how can I ignore the fact, having also read biographies of the author, that Dostoevsky's first wife was dying of tuberculosis in the next room as he wrote this deeply disturbing scene? Cruelly telling the prostitute how she will still be a sexual object for her clients despite coughing blood, the author could hear his wife coughing blood through the wall. This biographical "story"—the circumstances in which Dostoevsky wrote the work—frames and tenses the story on the page. The two unhappy circumstances call to each other. Critics can pretend to look at the actual printed book "purely," not knowing what we know, but at a psychological level our reaction to a text is inevitably coloured by such knowledge, if only because the wife's illness, and Dostoevsky's difficult relationship with her, feasibly has to do with the frighteningly negative energy coming off the page in *Notes*; this is the unhappy world this fiction leads me into.

Then one says that a published book is addressed to everyone, not to family and friends—but everyone where, everyone when? Certainly not those in the past, who are dead and cannot read it. Perhaps not those in distant lands and cultures, or in the distant future, whose opinions and attitudes the author doesn't know and cannot easily be in relation to. *Everyone*, in fact, means that public the author thinks of as his, the people he assumes, even if he never actually spends time thinking about it, will be reading his book (what the structuralists called "the implicit reader"). Not that an author will mind if the book is read by those it wasn't addressed to, but some notion of a public addressed seems an inevitable corollary of any utterance. "I've just done the last proofs of Lady C [*Lady Chatterley's Lover*]," D. H. Lawrence wrote in 1928. "I *hope* it'll make 'em howl—and let 'em do their paltry damnedest, after."[2] In this case "them" was more or less everybody in the British establishment. *They* were the people it was addressed to, aimed at, not us, not the German or Italian public, not a twenty-first-century student in Korea writing a doctoral thesis on D. H. Lawrence (curiously there have been any number of doctoral theses on Lawrence in Korea).

If we are *overhearing* Lawrence's argument with his English contemporaries, then a little knowledge about them and him will presumably give the argument and the novel more sense. The same will be true of the author's social set, and his family. Or rather, the more the book interests us the more we will be drawn to ask questions about that argument, that context, these dealings. When Beckett's Molloy remarks that he keeps warm in winter by wrapping himself in newspapers, then adds, "The Times Literary Supplement was admirably adapted to this purpose, of a never failing toughness and impermeability. Even farts made no impression on it,"[3] he is clearly taking a shot at the exclusiveness of the literary establishment as it was in his time (an establishment which had excluded him for so long), but in a way so much more elusive and melancholy and witty than Lawrence, especially when one thinks that the original *Molloy* was written in French and has "Le Supplément Littéraire du Times était excellent à cet effet, d'une solidité et non-porosité à toute épreuve. Les pets ne le dechi-raient pas."[4] It is rather as if Beckett wants to communicate something and at the same time *not* communicate it, not have it fall into the hands of those whom he means to criticize. He does not, now he is writing in French, redirect his satire to a French target. The object is ever the British literary establishment. But he is not even writing in their lan-guage, he will not give them the satisfaction of voicing his complaint directly, with the result that the remark becomes a joke shared with the French reader at the expense of the English establishment, and again a joke that reader could perhaps be forgiven for missing, so obliquely is it delivered. In any event, Beckett's is hardly a campaign to *change* that establishment; open warfare was simply not in his DNA as it was in Lawrence's. Noticeably, Beckett's fiction begins to include mother figures only after Beckett starts writing in French, which his mother couldn't read. Any biography of Beckett will indicate that this indirectness, which sometimes approaches, or wilfully aspires to, autism, was precisely his way of relating, or deliberately *not* relating to people, a strong behavioural pattern in his life.

Is it really, then, a retreat from the text to be interested in such pat-terns of behaviour, their coextension across work and life, or does it rather increase our engagement with the writing, making us more aware of how it operates, of its implications, of the way we react to it? Isn't it a natural response to our excitement over a work of art to want to understand more about its context? Paradoxically, we might say that writing a work of fiction, precisely because it gives the author the chance of denying any relationship between the story and real events, any intended message to those close to him, opens the way to sending far more powerful messages than he might ordinarily be able to or feel was wise.

Let's try now to give this mix of anecdotal evidence and general reflection some scientific dignity. My aim is to build up a simple theo-retical framework, based in large part on systemic psychology, that will allow us to explore a little further what happens when we come into contact with an author through his novels.

It was the British anthropologist Gregory Bateson who first sug-gested that personality differentiation, the process by which each of us establishes an identity both different from and in relation to those we live among, occurs around the behavioural polarities dominant in a given culture. Bateson had been observing the radically different behaviour patterns of men and women among the Iatmul Indians of Papua New Guinea. His aim was to get an insight into how a culture perpetuates itself while nevertheless allowing individuals a certain freedom within the shared collective ethos. After some time he realized that the Iatmul men tended to be exhibitionist and boastful while the women were quiet and admiring (of the men); indeed, the more the men were exhibitionist, the quieter and more contemplative the women became, to the point, in some cases, almost of catatonia. It was clear that the one behaviour pattern complemented and stimulated the other. So Bateson began to reflect that identity perhaps forms in a series of reactions to other standard behaviours within a culture, behaviours that necessarily channel and limit the possible responses.

As Bateson saw it, this process of reciprocally stimulated personality differentiation within a pre-existing framework—something he called schismogenesis—could be complementary or symmetrical. Among the Iatmul men the process is symmetrical: they are involved in a dynamic of escalating competition, each seeking to outdo the other in their exhibitionism to gain the women's attention. Between the men and women of the tribe, however, the process is complementary, each sex becoming ever more the opposite of the other.

Schismogenesis, as Bateson thought of it, was a powerful process and could be damaging, not only because it tended to violent extremes, but also because it could deny an individual any experience outside the particular behaviour pattern triggered by this social dynamic. He called his book on the Iatmul people *Naven* because this was the name of a bizarre series of rituals that he began to think of as "correcting" the schismogenetic process and fostering a general psychosocial stability. In these weirdly theatrical ceremonies men dressed up as women and vice versa. The women now assumed what was the traditional behaviour of their menfolk, boasting and making a great spectacle of themselves, while the men became abject and passive, to the point of submitting to simulated anal rape. Later, in studies made in Bali, Bateson posited the hypothesis that art, like ritual, might be a form of corrective to schismogenetic processes at work in society, a space that allowed people to explore different positions in relation to others from those they occupied in their everyday lives.

Bateson's initially simplistic model for exploring the interplay between individual and group, and its role in the formation of the individual, has since been developed by a number of behavioural psychologists interested in personality differentiation within families and larger groups and in the way the developing relationship between individual and group might lead to neurosis and mental illness. In particular, the Italian psychologist Valeria Ugazio introduced the notion that schismogenetic polarities have, as she put it, semantic content. Comparing themselves with others, she suggests, people can see themselves as fearful or courageous, selfish or altruistic, winners or losers, belonging to a peer group or not belonging, and so on. Around each of these polarities a process of schismogenesis could occur—faced with courage I vie to be more courageous, or grow fearful; seeing my brother's selfish behaviour, I am encouraged to behave unselfishly, or vice versa.

Ugazio argued that, although in any family a number of criteria for assessing others and ourselves will always be present, so that a child may be hearing one moment about courage or fear, and another about selfishness or altruism, and so on, nevertheless one polarity in particular will tend to dominate and to be considered the most important criterion for judging others, establishing the atmosphere and ethos of the group. As a consequence, in infancy and adolescence, family members will find themselves obliged to establish where they stand in relation to this criterion. Are they, in the end, winners or losers, do they see themselves as belonging or not belonging, good or bad, courageous or fearful?

In short, in any family each member from the very earliest age will be nudged towards an awareness of how they stand in relation to the value that most matters in the group. Consider, for example, a family that tends to talk about itself and others above all in terms of "dependence–independence." Drawing on thirty years' experience in family therapy, Ugazio offers these reflections in her book *Permitted and Forbidden Stories: Semantic Polarities and Psychopathologies in the Family*:

> In these families, conversations will tend to be organized around
> episodes where fear and courage, the need for protection and
> the desire for exploration play a central role . . . As a result of
> these conversational processes, members of these families will

feel, or be defined as, fearful or cautious or, alternatively, courageous, even reckless. They will find others prepared to protect
them, or alternatively people who are unable to survive without
their protection. They will marry partners who are fragile or
dependent, but also individuals who are free and sometimes
unwilling to make commitments. They will suffer for their
dependence. They will try in every way to gain their independence. In other cases they will be proud of their independence
and freedom, which they will defend more than everything else.
Admiration, contempt, conflict, alliances, love and hatred will
all be played out around issues of freedom/dependence.[5]

What Ugazio is suggesting is that people naturally tend to display
forms of behaviour that can be judged according to the criterion
dominant in the family or group, behaviour that "makes sense," negatively or positively, to those they have grown up with. If we are looking at a family that prizes belonging above all, its individual members
will be concerned with the nature of their inclusion in the group, the
rights of others to be included, the need to exclude this or that member, and so on. Ugazio writes:

The two main polarities are inclusion/exclusion, honour/dis-
grace. They are fuelled by joy/cheerfulness and anger/despair,
the emotions typifying these semantics. The most important
thing for members of these families is to be included as part of
the family, as well as being part of the wider community. The
reason is that within the same family group there are also those
who are excluded, marginalized or rejected. Expulsion from
the group, or not belonging to a family, is seen by such people as
an irreparable disgrace, whereas the greatest good is to be
well-established and respected within the groups to which they
belong, including family and community. Yet it is often in the
name of dignity that permanent rifts occur. Honour in these
families is therefore a value just as fundamental as belonging.
(Ugazio, 228)

It is hard reading this not to think of Dickens and his constant concern about the placing of his characters, and indeed himself, in and
out of families and clubs, prisons and institutions: the cheerfulness of

sitting around the family hearth at Christmas time (of which the reading experience itself is a part), the despair of being excluded from it.
And, in fact, Ugazio's adaptation of Bateson's thinking necessarily
leads her to a narrative vision of character development, to the point
that she occasionally draws on fiction to illustrate her ideas. So Dostoevsky's *Brothers Karamazov* is used as an example of a family where
behaviour is always seen in terms of good and evil, with good being
understood as altruistic renunciation and evil as selfish indulgence.
We have the saintly Alyosha, who appears to take after his dead
mother, the evil Dimitri who very obviously follows in his father's footsteps, and the more complex Ivan, who oscillates between the two
positions, doesn't know whether he is good or evil, and seems eager
to go beyond this choice, to be spared the necessity of making that
decision.

   This idea that in the process of polarization round certain values
someone will find it difficult to establish a stable position is central to
Ugazio's thesis, and indeed to the arguments that I will be putting
forward in this book about relationships between authors' lives and
the stories they write. But not to run ahead of ourselves, let us just say
for the moment that specific family contexts can all too often create
situations where one family member finds himself putting a supreme
value on independence, but is simultaneously extremely needy for
protection; or where a person who feels she must belong at all costs
also finds herself ashamed of the community she belongs to; or where
someone who absolutely must be able to think of himself as good
nevertheless cannot give up behaviour reckoned bad without experiencing feelings of deprivation and depression, etc.

   It should be clear that we're not talking about a "choice" of values
here, in the sense of a reasoned assessment of clearly defined criteria,
nor about incompetence, a failure to do something one should reason-
ably be able to do, but about a family narrative that anchors values to
relationships, emotions, and a unique personal history. Considering
the case history of a young man with a phobic disorder, for example,
Ugazio first describes his parents' relationship; the father has always
been an independent, enterprising man who started his own business,
travels widely, and takes risks. For her part, his wife is happy to admire
her husband and to stay at home looking after their children. Her
yearning for a safe environment is met by her partner's courage and

fortitude, while his self esteem is bolstered by his wife's admiration and dependence. All is well. Now three children arrive. The first, a girl, follows in her father's footsteps. She travels, gets herself a prestigious boyfriend, leaves him, finds a job abroad—in short, establishes her independence. Her younger brother does the same. He loves extreme sports, has a girlfriend, but postpones any idea of living with her, not wanting, he says, to be "trapped."

The third child, another boy, is more attached to his mother. She has drawn him closer to her, perhaps a little weary now of her husband's constant travelling, his triumphant independence, and the son has grown closer to her, if only in an attempt to distinguish himself from his older brother and sister who are closer to their father. When this third boy reaches adolescence, however, he begins to appreciate that though he enjoys a special relationship with his mother, nevertheless her real admiration goes to the values of independence and courage embodied by his father and siblings. This new awareness is disturbing. The boy now tries to show his independence, choosing to study far from home; but as soon as he is away he feels he has taken on more than he can handle, missing the protection of home. So he returns home earlier than he meant to for a break, but now finds that however initially reassuring home may be, his relationship with his mother is undermining his self esteem. It is she who makes him fearful. He is suffocating. Growing older, the same ambivalence is repeated in his relationship with his girlfriend: he enjoys the security and affection she offers, yet simultaneously these positive feelings are experienced as humiliating and imprisoning. By the time the young man decides to go to the therapist he is having panic attacks every time he leaves home and vomiting as soon as he returns.

One of the implications of the systemic school of psychology, which was further developed by the so-called positional theorists, is that there is no clear line between mental illness and normality. To a certain degree most people will feel at least some tension between competing values and many will need to cast about for life strategies, and indeed stories of themselves, that allow them to find stability where there is possible conflict and breakdown. One classic is the "good" person who only "sins" when away from home, where his behaviour will not upset loved ones; another the fearful person who achieves a sense of self esteem by showing courage in carefully circumscribed situations, the football stadium, an extreme sport, some cultural activity. Ugazio has dozens of examples of stratagems that acknowledge the pull of both sides of a polarity; however, most interesting among them for our purposes is her reflection that intellectual activity and particularly creative activity can prove helpful in certain situations for reconciling conflicting values. The person who feels they must be good, despite the fact that renunciation of pleasure brings on a sense of desolation, can indulge a range of transgressive experiences vicariously by writing a certain kind of story while still feeling that the overall enterprise (of writing) is "good." The fearful person desirous of independence can feel courageous and independent *on the page*, if not perhaps in life. As we will see, this was very much the case with Thomas Hardy.

To recap, Bateson, Ugazio, and other psychologists who have looked at identity as a matter of positioning oneself within pre-existing groups and behaviour patterns, offer a model that proposes that for each of us certain values are predominant, and that this dominance tends to favour the emergence of certain kinds of characters and stories and to discourage others. The suggestion is that however creative they may be we can expect a certain constancy, continuity and, if we can put it this way, a *fertile limitation* in the works of most storytellers; their stories will tend to be of a certain kind and, whatever the setting or genre, to revolve around the same values. Empirically, this fits with our sense, when we read a number of novels by the same author, that the characters form a sort of extended family across the oeuvre as a whole. Not that an author will not develop new characters from time to time, but that in their preoccupations and mannerisms and vision they will stand in evident *relation* to the other characters; an emotional tone is established, that may intensify or grow more complex but nevertheless is such that we would not be surprised if a character from one book didn't turn up in the pages of another. And, of course, some authors do allow this to happen. One thinks of Faulkner, Joyce, Hardy, Beckett, Woolf, more recently Philip Roth. If we turn, then, from the work to the author's life we find that the same kind of stories occur, the same kinds of judgements are made of people, the same emotional tone exists, in their own relationships. The scene of the older Dickens meeting the young American girl on the train and indulging her is absolutely in line with any number of encounters between older benefactors and adolescent girls in his novels.

Ugazio, as I have said, suggests that the practice of creating art, and narrative in particular, can be a way of responding to difficulties in finding a position in the force field of values in which the artist grew up. This is in line with our sense that many of our authors are/were, to say the least, troubled people, and recalls the old intuition that there is an affinity between certain forms of mental disturbance and creativity. Ivan, in *The Brothers Karamazov*, finds it difficult to establish a stable position in the world of good and evil as his family and society conceive it for him, and Ivan is evidently the closest figure in the book to being Dostoevsky's alter ego; he is, as it were, the writer figure. Dostoevsky himself, as we know, oscillated between sprees of gambling and extramarital affairs on the one hand and a desire to be saintly and assist his family and his beloved Mother Russia on the other. We could say that his novel allows for an exploration of "evil" experience within a reassuring overall framework of Christian morality that is strongly, even wilfully asserted at the end of the story.

All this suggests a relationship between the author and his or her book and between the book and the world that is rather more intriguing than that offered by the "biographical fallacy" as earlier defined. Rather than "reducing" the novel to those elements that reproduce or camouflage events in the author's life, the narrative itself, the stories it offers and the style in which they are set down, is understood within the general dynamic of the writer's behaviour, the way he or she deals with the world. We can, if we like, reflect on projections of the kinds of dilemmas the author faced within the novel, but we can also see the work itself, the provocations it offers, the conclusions it draws, as attempts to shift or stabilize the author's position in relation to those around him, or even his image of himself.

Let us now take this a step further and talk about the relationship between author and reader as it forms in the space of the story.

One of the ideas Ugazio draws from her model is that misunderstandings between people, not simple semantic misunderstandings but the deeper confusion that comes from feeling that a new friend or partner has behaved in a way that is inexplicable, may arise where personalities have been formed in quite different family contexts. She calls these moments of misunderstanding "enigmatic episodes" and offers as an example the relationship between Franz and Sabina in Milan Kundera's novel *The Unbearable Lightness of Being*.

[Franz and Sabina's] relationship is marked from the very beginning by enigmatic episodes: Kundera calls them "words misunderstood" and develops a short glossary of them. Let us recall a few of them.

Sabina asked Franz at a certain point: "Why don't you sometimes use your strength on me?" Franz replied: "Because love means relinquishing strength." And Sabina realized two things: firstly, that Franz's words were noble and just; secondly, that with these words Franz disqualified himself in her eyes as a sexual partner.

Franz often told Sabina about his mother, perhaps with a sort of unconscious calculation. He imagined that Sabina would be attracted by his capacity for faithfulness and thus would have been won over by him. Franz did not know that Sabina was attracted by betrayal, and not by faithfulness.

When Sabina told him once about her walks in cemeteries, Franz shuddered with disgust. For him, cemeteries were "bone and stone dumps," but for her they provided the only nostalgic memory of her country of birth, Bohemia.

Franz admired Sabina's homeland. When she told him about herself and her Czech friends, Franz heard the words prison, persecution, tanks in the streets, emigration, posters and banned literature, and Sabina appeared even more beautiful because behind her he could glimpse the painful drama of her country . . . Sabina felt no love for that drama. Prison, persecution, banned books, occupation and tanks were ugly words to her, devoid of the slightest romantic intrigue. (Ugazio, 62)

To use the jargon of this branch of psychology, Franz and Sabina find it difficult to "co-position" themselves the one to the other because neither can understand the stance the other adopts over certain issues. It is not simply that they disagree, which would be easy, rather neither knows where the other is coming from.

As the novel develops, Kundera shows how the reactions prompted in the two by these words and issues in fact arise from the different family backgrounds and life experiences in which they have grown to maturity, each with quite different criteria for assessing behaviour. In order, then, for the relationship to continue despite these enigmatic episodes, there has to be a strong gratification and, in the long term, an overcoming of misunderstanding through change, through appreciating, in this case, that graveyards or revolution might be seen in a different way, or more problematically that betrayal might be experienced in a different way. But since change, as Ugazio remarks, is hardly at a premium on most people's agendas, a relationship where enigmatic episodes are frequent will tend to be brief, since "we prefer to 'co-position' with people and in interactive situations that do not place our identity in doubt."

Let us now make a move that Ugazio does not make. What if we consider our immersion in a book as a meeting with a person who may or may not share the value system we live in, a relationship that may have enigmatic episodes, parts of the story, reflections, descriptions, that hardly make sense to us; or again, stories that confirm, one hundred per cent, the kind of world we feel we live in, even though perhaps we disagree with the author's position in relation to that world?

In the case of Franz and Sabina, the relationship survives for some time despite their misunderstandings largely thanks to the erotic charge between them and the fascination of each for the exoticism of the other. Let's say that when reading novels this kind of charge, the pleasure that makes the continuation of a difficult relationship possible, might most simply be provided by the seductive element of the plot, the invitation to identify with the characters, the eloquence of the style. So we continue to read, for a while, even when the behaviour of our characters or the descriptions and reflections of the narrator, or the whole method of proceeding, may seem bewildering and alienating. However, if the enigmatic episodes become too many, or if the plot lags, or our emotional engagement with the characters fades, we may terminate the relationship and put the book down. We couldn't get on with the author, we say, he was coming out of left field, he or she meant nothing to us (I had an experience like this recently with the German author Jenny Erpenbeck). Usually the reader will describe this breakdown in terms of a failure of competence on the author's part. If the author is highly praised by people we respect (as is my case with Erpenbeck), we may take refuge in notions of taste; this is not the kind of book we like, and so on. What I am suggesting, however, is that this reluctance to continue with a novel is possibly not dissimilar to the way we choose not to pursue an acquaintance with someone whose behaviour we find unnerving and inexplicable. We don't know how to gel with them. They make no sense to us.

Again and again reviewer reactions to novels suggest that the reader has experienced something analogous to Ugazio's enigmatic episodes. In the reviewer's case, since reading to the end of the book is a duty, rather than a pleasure, exasperation is likely to be greater if these episodes are too frequent. Here is Middleton Murry writing about D. H. Lawrence.

> *Women in Love* is five hundred pages of passionate vehemence, wave after wave of turgid, exasperated writing impelled towards some distant and invisible end; the persistent underground beating of some dark and inaccessible sea in an underworld whose inhabitants are known by this alone, that they writhe continually, like the damned, in a frenzy of sexual awareness of one another. Their creator believes that he can distinguish the writhing of one from the writhing of another . . . to him they are utterly and profoundly different; to us they are all the same.[6]

Murry cannot see what differentiates Lawrence's characters, hence the melodrama makes no sense and the plot becomes tedious. In a later chapter I hope I can show that we only need appreciate the dominant semantic in Lawrence's work (and life) for the differences between the characters to become clear to the point of over-definition and the sense of the drama obvious and urgent. However, that Murry misses this is not due to any lack of intelligence or reading acumen— Murry was a fine critic—but to his moving in a quite different world of values; he has never seen anything like this before, it is a serious challenge to his way of thinking about life. The same is true of the critic who has this to say about Hardy's *The Return of the Native*:

> Mr. Hardy's tragedy seems carefully limited to gloom. It gives us the measure of human miserableness, rather than of human grief—of the incapacity of man to be great in suffering, or anything else, rather than of his greatness in suffering . . . The hero's agony is pure, unalloyed misery, not grief of the deepest and noblest type, which can see a hope in the future and repent the errors of the past.[7]

As so often with Victorian critics, a prescriptive note creeps in, which again is in line with words like "repent." At another moment in the review, considering the character of Eustacia, the rather bold, rash female protagonist of the story, the reviewer expresses a perplexity that suggests the difficulty of someone used to thinking of life in terms of good and evil trying to get to grips with an author and a character who have quite other values in mind. This actually pushes the reviewer to use an oxymoron, clear sign that he is moving into an area of difficulty:

> [Hardy's] coldly passionate heroine, Eustacia Vye, never reproaches herself for a moment with the inconstancy and poverty of her own affections. On the contrary, she has no feeling that anything which happens within her has relation to right and wrong at all, or that such a thing as responsibility exists. (*Native*, 424)

Here the reviewer is perfectly accurate. But whereas Hardy has no difficulty taking an amoral person like Eustacia seriously and considering her as a worthy heroine for his novel, the reviewer can only categorize such a character in the negative side of the good/evil spectrum; for him she is merely selfish; consequently he can't understand why Hardy is spending so much time trying to enlist our sympathy for the woman. Needless to say, the reviewer then transforms this sense that there is something he can't accept in the book into an aesthetic criticism appealing to traditional notions of what "tragedy" should be and complaining that Hardy has got his formula wrong; he should have created more noble characters. In fact, Hardy is simply not interested in good and evil, or noble characters, but entirely focused on the kind of emotional world that forms around issues of courage and fear, liberty and constriction. If he introduced the kind of hero the reviewer wants, the whole plot would disappear in a trice. But Hardy would never have dreamed of introducing such a character and quite likely would have been unable to do so.

By suggesting, then, that our encounter with a novel has analogies with meeting another person, I am proposing that the whole issue of liking and disliking is more complex than is usually supposed by a tradition of literary criticism that focuses entirely on questions of aesthetics and morals. I am also appealing directly to our experience of reading, rather than to any theory about texts applied in the laboratories of academe. A book exists actively when it is read, hence the reactions of readers will tell us a great deal about it. It is perfectly possible, for example, in my experience, to have the lowest opinion of the quality of a novel, in terms of writing, style, structure, etc., and yet to be riveted by the story it tells, perhaps because it intersects with the kind of world we move in, hence it immediately matters to us, we recognize what is at stake. Vice versa, it is possible to be extremely impressed by the quality of the writing in a book and quite indifferent to the way it develops, even to put it down half-way through and think no more of it.

So far I have presented the idea of the enigmatic episode as an experience that is invariably negative, as if what we wanted was *always* to find confirmation that the world is as we believe it is. This is not the case, and particularly not the case when we're reading; some incomprehension can be exciting and, despite my analogy between reading and real-life encounters, our engagement with a novel is, or can easily seem to be, a more leisurely and controllable experience than, say, discussing betrayal with a partner. It is not immediately so dangerous, it does not so immediately impact on our lives. On the page, we can afford to linger over ideas and relationships and reactions that seem quite new and even disorientating to us. When, in *Women in Love*, Gudrun slaps Gerald across the face quite unexpectedly during their first really private meeting, we may be bewildered, we may or may not be aware that we are being invited into a world of feeling that is strange to us (though not of course to all of us), the kind of relationship that Lawrence knows all about and we do not; but we can always put the book down a while and reflect, we can take it page by page. We personally have not been slapped in the face. Maybe at the end of the book we will have allowed ourselves to open up a little to a play of emotional forces that would otherwise have remained obscure to us, so that that slap may even begin to make sense to us. An enigmatic episode can be a moment of growth, a moment that allows us to become aware of the boundaries and possibly limits of our own emotional world. Kundera's lovers Franz and Sabina break up. There is too much that divides them. All the same, those misunderstandings have taught them something. Some time after the relationship ended, we hear this of Sabina:

> Suddenly she missed Franz terribly. When she told him about
> her cemetery walks, he gave a shiver of disgust and called
> cemeteries bone and stone dumps. A gulf of misunderstanding
> had immediately opened between them. Not until that day at
> the Montparnasse Cemetery did she see what he meant. She
> was sorry to have been so impatient with him. Perhaps if they
> had stayed together longer, Sabina and Franz would have begun
> to understand the words they used. (Ugazio, 65)

Ugazio herself talks of psychotherapy as a process where enigmatic
episodes are deliberately created by therapists for patients in carefully
controlled circumstances and with the emotional charge necessarily
present in a session of psychotherapy in order to invite them away
from the conflict of values in which they are enmired towards some
different vision of life, a system of values within which they might
more easily find a stable position. In this case of course the experience
is enigmatic only on the side of the patient, who doesn't understand
why the therapist has reacted in the way he or she has. In fiction, too,
much will depend on how we respond to certain challenges as the
narrative develops in unexpected ways, and this will largely depend on
the amount of emotional involvement the author has managed to
establish before the going gets tough.

Think of a writer like Beckett, very widely known to theatre goers,
but much less to novel readers, despite the fact that Beckett considered
the plays minor works compared to the novels, potboilers almost—
and certainly hardcore Beckett fans (myself included) tend to feel the
same. However, for most readers new to Beckett the novels present
themselves as one long bewildering enigmatic episode. It is all too easy
in these circumstances to put the book down. There is just not enough
pleasure generated in the traditional way to encourage us to overcome
the incomprehension.

In the theatre the situation is quite different. The flesh-and-blood
presence of the actors on stage creates a sense of reality and possible
identification that the absurd plots and dialogues then comically
undermine, so that the tension behind all of Beckett's work between
affirmation of reality and denial of reality is dramatized for us in the
contrast between the believable actor and the inexplicable, disorienting world he is in. At the same time, the social conventions of the

theatre which trap us respectfully together in an intimate space for a pre-established time, make it far more likely that the sceptical neophyte will follow a Beckett work from beginning to end, have time to be enchanted by the rhythms of his writing and begin to understand the relationship of what he sees and hears to a recognizable human condition. If few readers get through *The Unnameable* or *How It Is*, almost everybody can watch *Godot* to the final curtain. In short, the emotional experience of *being in the theatre* provides the impetus necessary for tackling the enigma that Beckett's work presents for most of us on first meeting. Similarly, there are people one only begins to appreciate as interesting when circumstances force us to spend a long time in their company, at work in the office, perhaps, or on a long journey. In the case of Beckett the payoff is considerable and may even shift a person's entire vision of life. In this regard, one sees how this approach to novels is in line with the common-sense view that there are certain works that allow "easy entry" to a particular author. "Which book should I start with?" is an intelligent question when facing a complex author, and getting that choice right can determine whether one goes on to read the author with profit. To begin Beckett with *How It Is* would probably mean never reading Beckett at all.

So if we are eager to convince ourselves that fiction and narrative are essentially positive and even therapeutic, we could now stop and say that novels offer both a moment of relief—allowing us to reposition ourselves in a world which is not our own, in line with Bateson's vision of certain functions of ritual and art—and again a moment of growth as we allow ourselves to take on board and give credit to an action or behaviour pattern that perhaps in ordinary life might have had us turning our backs at once. In this scenario literature could be seen as a useful instrument in overcoming prejudice.

But to rush to this conclusion would only be to reveal our own anxiety that our reading habit or writing habit be inscribed as necessarily "good." It would be more realistic surely to acknowledge that just as a meeting with another person can have positive or negative consequences, so likewise can fiction, depending on the reader's relation to the writing. An accomplished writer can draw us very powerfully toward positions that could be harmful to us. When we pick up a writer of the power of Thomas Bernhard, for example, it may quickly seem to us that his constant sense of outrage is really the *only* way of viewing the world; it may seem after we have put the book down that we are living and moving in the world as Bernhard sees it. Certainly, many writers have succumbed for years to Bernhard's influence to the point of offering stories of their own that feel like mechanical reproductions of Bernhard's rhetoric and vision. They may even assume his posturing and pessimism. They may even change the way they relate to other people they know. Bernhard does everything he can to warn us of the persuasive and coercive powers of charismatic figures, great art and great writing, but nevertheless his books do have that persuasive power. They are not innocuous. Likewise one would not want to give one of Thomas Hardy's later novels to somebody about to marry or planning a child, since the essential message of those narratives, however brilliant they may be, is that whatever can go wrong will and that every ambitious enterprise will backfire.

To summarize: for those who indulge these habits, writing and reading fiction are part of the whole business of living and becoming, establishing and maintaining an identity, a position in relation to others and the world. For the novelist the text is absolutely integrated in his life and circumstances; what he writes comes out of and rebounds back on his mental life, his private life, his professional life. It is something dense and complex in which much is at stake. When the reader moves into this force field, he may find things that reinforce his own vision of the world in ways that are gratifying or perhaps suffocating, that make him happy or angry, or alternatively he may be disorientated in ways that are exciting or disturbing, or seriously challenging to the way he lives. In this regard, acquiring experience of reading and spending some time thinking about the way our minds engage with narrative fiction may give the reader tools for growth in some circumstances, and in others a means for protecting himself. If unprepared, one can find oneself unsettled and threatened.

When it comes to writing and reading, then, one has to accept that there is a huge range of intention and experience behind what might at first glance seem a uniform phenomenon. A writer can decide to be strictly formulaic, aiming absolutely at a standard, genre form of entertainment, perhaps writing romances for Harlequin books, who distribute guidelines to authors suggesting how plots should develop in this or that kind of romance. Even so, I doubt if the writer will be able to keep life and work entirely separate. Merely the choice of this sort of book, the renunciation of a more ambitious kind of writing, and then the way he or she works in that chosen genre, will begin to be important for the writer in terms of identity and will affect those around him or her.

Readers too, if they so desire, may choose to read only what is absolutely safe to them, books they have already read before in a way; this is the logic, after all, behind those Harlequin romances, or certain kinds of detective story: to offer the reader an encounter free of any kind of enigmatic episode, the schematic nature of the cover being a guarantee of the kind of experience proposed. But even the repeated use of a narcotic is part of a life experience and can lead to satiation or depression.

What I am rejecting, then, is the notion that writing can be removed from life to be dissected in the realms of academe as something separate from writer and reader, like some sort of specimen nailed to the neutral territory of the scientist's laboratory bench. Indeed, even to think that such a thing could be done suggests a certain psychological make-up on the part of the critic, a desire for the protection of a circumscribed environment where he has complete control. A critic who excludes from his work any reflection of how the texts he considers affect him, *personally*, of how he stands in relation to them *personally*, is, as I see it, living in denial of the very experience that he is looking to for a meal ticket. An anthropological study of literary academe, the kind of person it attracts and the behaviour patterns it perpetuates, is long overdue.

The regular reader who is not a critic proceeds in a different way and is rarely sufficiently interested to read an entire essay of literary criticism, never mind a book, since as a rule such criticism says so little about the experience of reading. He, or more often she, reads a novel because it impresses and interests him/her, because it engages with his or her life. Let's imagine a young woman picking up a book by Philip Roth in the 1970s. The book talks about marriage and affairs. It takes an unconventional and aggressive point of view. She is taken by his point of view, though perhaps not in agreement with it. She reads another by the same author. Then another. Over twenty years she may read five or six works by Roth. She is aware of the continuity of tone and content between those works. Her newspapers give her some news of Roth's life, which, since she now knows his books, she reads with interest. She understands that there is a tension between a desire for complete sexual freedom and an awareness of the price society exacts for that freedom, so that desire and fear are in constant tension; she understands that there are elements in Roth's life that stand in obvious relation to his novels, that these subjects are urgent personal questions for him. Maybe they are for her too. Or for people she knows. Maybe she doesn't "agree" with Roth at all, even finds him offensive, but nevertheless tells herself it is useful to understand how men like Roth think. When she sees a new novel by Roth in the bookshops, she wants to find out "where he is up to" with these questions, whether he has reached a point of resolution, whether he has a new perspective on these old problems. Even if a new novel does not entirely convince her—in fact, had it been the first she had tackled by the author she might not have finished it—nevertheless she is intrigued by its relation to the previous novels and by the area of speculation it opens up for her on how Roth is pursuing his reflections on eroticism and betrayal and society into old age. The author's protagonists, she observes, tend to age in line with their creator. And of course she too is ageing.

At this point we can say that Roth has entered her life and that the works cannot be considered singly, nor separately from the Roth, real or otherwise, that she has encountered in the media—a TV interview perhaps, a feature in the Sunday papers. Her awareness that this material probably offers only a very incomplete picture of his life actually increases her interest. She doesn't yet know everything. Thus, over thirty years, we have something analogous to an extended conversation. Our reader knows what kind of world awaits her when she reads Roth, but she knows that the novels are never quite the same, since Roth seems unable to find a stable position between the demands of Eros and the social realities that surround sexual experience. She can expect tension, humour, genuine exploration. And she reads on. When she hears, in 2013, that Roth has said he will not write any more she feels vaguely bereft. Is it that he has stopped writing because age has finally got the better of his libido? Perhaps at this point she picks up a biography, or she rereads one or two of his books. She does not want to let this story go.

I am not saying that this experience, where text and biography are now inextricably mixed is *preferable* or *superior* to the one-off encounter with a fine novel about whose author we know nothing; I am simply inviting you to consider that this is the experience of reading that many people have and that drives the market for fiction, particularly serious fiction. We involve ourselves in ongoing relationships with writers and position ourselves in relation to them and the kind of stories they tell, much as we position ourselves in relation to the people we meet and know. Writing and reading are part of the immensely complex business of being ourselves.

Notes

1. See the University of Houston website <http://coursesite.uhcl.edu/HSH/Whitec/terms/B/BiographFallacy.htm>. The definition is repeated on many internet sites.
2. *The Letters of D. H. Lawrence*, ed. James T. Boulton (Cambridge University Press, 2000), 114.
3. Samuel Beckett, *Molloy*, English edition (London: Jupiter Books, Calder & Boyars, 1971), 31.
4. Samuel Beckett, *Molloy*, French edition (Paris: Éditions de Minuit, 1951), 39.
5. Valeria Ugazio, *Permitted and Forbidden Stories: Semantic Polarities and Psychopathologies in the Family*, trans. Richard Dixon (New York: Routledge, 2013), 84. Hereafter cited as "Ugazio."
6. John Middleton Murry: "The Nostalgia of Mr D. H. Lawrence," *Nation and Athenaeum*, 13 August 1921.
7. Unsigned review from the *Spectator*, 8 February 1879, quoted in Thomas Hardy, *The Return of the Native*, ed. Simon Avery (Toronto: Broadview, 2013), 425. Hereafter cited as "*Native*" with volume and chapter references.

3

Joyce

A Winner Looking to Lose

> The reason why these families give particular attention to the
> winner/loser polarity is often attributed to a *history of social
> downfall and recovery or to class differences between the original families
> from which the partners come*...The range of emotional states
> typically experienced...includes boasting, a feeling of personal
> effectiveness and skill, command, control and self-confidence
> against shame, humiliation, impotence or inadequacy. Jealousy,
> envy and rivalry are naturally part of the daily emotional
> experience within these families.
>
> Valeria Ugazio, *Permitted and Forbidden Stories*, 182.

Let's now return to our initial sketches of possible meetings with celebrated authors and see if we can draw on the material of the previous
chapter to transform those lightweight provocations into something
more substantial. What is this strange trajectory of Joyce's work all
about; the constant focus on Dublin, but in a style that is ever more
experimental and taxing until we reach a point where the manner of
the writing seems more remarkable than the place or people described?
If we understood that trajectory, would we have understood Joyce, his
work, and our reaction to it?

Born in 1882, James Augustine Aloysius Joyce was the first surviving child of John and May Joyce (née Murry) whose recent marriage
had been fiercely and bitterly opposed by the parents of both partners; the Joyces because the Murrys were of a lower class, the Murrys
because John Joyce was not considered of good character. There
was a previous baby, named after John, who had died at barely two
months. The first healthy son was thus a crucial affirmation of the

marriage and, despite thirteen further births producing nine surviving children, James would always be his father's favourite and was
always encouraged to believe he was destined for greatness. John
Joyce would do anything for James, recalled his sister Eileen, even if
it meant the other children went without. And still they all loved him.
When, aged 10, James wrote a poem about the betrayal and downfall
of the Irish leader Parnell, his father, an avid supporter of republicanism and Parnell in particular, had dozens of copies made to circulate
among friends. Young James was a precocious success writing about
a tragic defeat.

To be singled out for glory will mean different things depending on
the character and achievements of the person who is singling you out.
By far the most important formative influence on James's life, John
Joyce can best be described as a *spectacular* failure, a man whose descent
into alcoholism and poverty during James's adolescence commanded
the appalled attention of all around him. They were many. A talented
singer and raconteur, hard-drinking and gregarious, John spent count-
less hours in Dublin pubs drinking away a considerable inheritance
(the family had owned a number of properties in Cork) and neglecting
the duties he had been assigned by the various government depart-
ments that hired and invariably fired him. He was well known, well
loved, and beyond help. The impression one has of him from biographies and from Joyce's descriptions of Simon Dedalus, the character
based on his father in the avowedly autobiographical *A Portrait of the
Artist as a Young Man*, is of a patriarch who, while singing his son's
praises, is himself such a dominating, magnetic, and boastful presence
that it is hard to imagine anyone finding space beside him. Here he is
in *A Portrait*, talking to pub acquaintances in his son's presence.

By God, I don't feel more than eighteen myself. There's that son
of mine there not half my age and I'm a better man than he is
any day of the week.

—Draw it mild now, Dedalus. I think it's time for you to take
a back seat, said the gentleman who had spoken before.

—No, by God! asserted Mr Dedalus. I'll sing a tenor song
against him or I'll vault a five-barred gate against him or I'll run
with him after the hounds across the country as I did thirty
years ago along with the Kerry Boy and the best man for it.

—But he'll beat you here, said the little old man, tapping his
forehead and raising his glass to drain it.[1]

The father has previously been boastful *of* the son, but in part to raise
his own self esteem, which he now pits *against* the boy, sure that, physically, he has the beating of him; others are aware, however, that when
it comes to intellect the boy will win out. So even if it wasn't perhaps
immediately clear to James, as a child, what being a success in the
vicinity of John Joyce and *for* John Joyce might entail, he would nevertheless soon have grasped that the winning strategy must be to privi-
lege the intellectual life over the physical. Nothing is clearer in Joyce's
writings, in their up-front sophistication and increasingly elaborate
style, than their intellectual quality, even though very often what is
spoken about is the physicality of the body. Physicality, we might say,
is possessed, intellectually.

James's infancy and adolescence were spent in two sharply contrasting environments: rigidly organized, hierarchical Catholic boarding
schools and a turbulent, overcrowded, argumentative family that was
more and more frequently obliged to move house as John Joyce took
pride in cheating landlords by decamping without paying rent, as if the
relationship between owner and tenant was not a moral obligation,
but a battle of wits. Of course the need to move was a defeat—John
was out of pocket again—but within the general debacle avoiding the
rent was a victory. With ten children the logistics of these moonlight
flits must have been complicated indeed.

In this troubled, multitudinous family, these severe and regimented
schools, what space or place was there for a boy destined for greatness? Written and rewritten through his twenties and early thirties, *A
Portrait of the Artist as a Young Man* shows the author's alter ego forming
around predicaments of positioning. To an extraordinary degree it is
as if identity were always a question of measuring yourself in relation
to and often against someone else.

In the opening lines of the novel Stephen is centre stage in the story
his father tells him. The first words of the book are spoken for him, a
song is sung for him, his father looks through a magnifying glass at
him; he is larger than life. On the same page, however, he is obliged to
hide under the table as his mother and aunt demand confessions and
conformity. He must apologize or lose his eyes. Sight is always the

physical weak point, for Joyce and for Stephen, the cause of possible defeat.

On page two, frightened by the action on the school rugby field, the young Stephen lingers on "the fringe of his line," separate from the others, but mulling over the names of various items of rugby kit, other boys' nicknames, things people say. During lessons he keeps his head down, merely feigning participation to avoid punishment. He considers words he has written by a map of the world in his geography book.

Stephen Dedalus
Class of Elements
Clongowes Wood College
Sallins
County Kildare
Ireland
Europe
The World
The Universe

However, this confident opening outwards from the local to the universal is threatened by the incursion of another boy, Fleming, who has scribbled some doggerel in Stephen's book that confines him, Stephen, in the conventional, nationalist/catholic scheme of things.

Stephen Dedalus is my name,
Ireland is my nation.
Clongowes is my dwellingplace
And heaven my expectation.

So a place in the free open universe merges into rivalry with an invasive companion.

In these opening pages of *A Portrait* a constant sense of vulnerability resulting from physical frailty and weak eyesight leads Stephen to cultivate a withdrawn mental space where he focuses on the language the other boys use, simultaneously feeding on their energy and detaching himself from them. But weakness and withdrawal invite enemies; a boy pushes him in a ditch, he catches a cold. Finally we find the one place at school where Stephen is really happy: the sick bay. Removed from the hurly burly of class and playing field, he fantasizes his own death, the remorse of the enemies who hurt him, the regret of his parents. Now language embellishes and consoles:

> How beautiful and sad that was! How beautiful the words were...(chapter 1)

Soon he is comparing his own imagined death with Parnell's; he has been treacherously used and isolated, as was Parnell; like the great Parnell he will die and this will place him at the centre of everybody's attention. In a way death will be a success in that everybody will be sorry he is gone. Greatness and defeat are superimposed, at least when language is used poetically.

We hardly need to worry whether these events in *A Portrait* are *true*: it is the pattern of behaviour that matters: vulnerability prompts detachment achieved through a focus on language, often the sound and the rhythm, the mechanics of the words, rather than their content, after which a poetic manipulation of language brings consolation and a sense of superiority and belonging at a distance. It is important for Joyce to give the maximum value to language since that will be the instrument of his passing from weak boy on the side-lines of the rugby field, dominated by figures like his robust father, to superior figure playing a game all his own. "Joyce seemed to think that words were omnipotent," Huxley noted years later. "They are not" (Bowker, 339).

At school in his teens, Joyce found an easy way of belonging: religious devotion; but also a way of distinguishing himself, by pushing devotion to the limit, writing religious verse and toying with thoughts of the priesthood, something his mother would have appreciated. Much is made of the adolescent Joyce's swings between extremes of religious and profane behaviour, moving from brothels and drunkenness to marathons with the rosary; however, there is nothing in the biographies to suggest a deeply-felt religious dilemma or profound sense of guilt. Rather the boy strives to outdo the others in every area where he feels he can compete. When he is religious his devotions are extreme, his rosaries long and meticulous; when he is depraved his depravity likewise. What tempts him in the priesthood is the priest's power over human souls; what characterizes relations with prostitutes is the obvious hierarchy guaranteed by payment. Meantime, each type of involvement, religious or profane, allows him to explore a social situation and above all to master its language, pushing his behaviour to the limit before moving on. After rejecting religion in his late teens and refusing in 1903 to take mass in obedience to his dying mother, Joyce nevertheless continued to be a church goer who now made himself conspicuous by not taking mass.

The trick of being simultaneously inside and outside the group is most evident with Joyce's singing. Sharing his father's talent, Joyce loved to perform wherever possible. Irish ballads. Immersed in the music, he was as Irish as one can be, but in a way that required neither interaction nor submission. For preference he sang alone and, following in his father footsteps, always thought of singing as a competition.

Here, in the words of the diarist Joseph Holloway, is the 22-year-old Joyce taking centre stage to sing, before withdrawing to his own special space:

> Mr J. Joyce, a (mysterious kind of) strangely aloof, silent youth, with weird, penetrating, large eyes, which he frequently shaded with his hand and with a half-bashful, far-away expression on his face, sang some dainty old world ballads most artistically and pleasingly, some to his own accompaniment. As he sings he sways his head from side to side to add to the soulfulness of his rendering. Later he sat in a corner and gazed at us all in turn in an uncomfortable way from under his brows and said little or nothing all evening. (Bowker, 121)

The description recalls these lines from *A Portrait*, lines the diary writer couldn't have known about, because as yet unwritten:

> But when he had sung his song and withdrawn into a snug corner of the room he began to taste the joy of his loneliness. (chapter 2)

On this occasion, in the novel, withdrawal wins him the attention of the girl he is interested in who becomes curious about his apartness. It is a winning position. But Joyce wasn't always a winner. At a major singing competition in 1904 he was denied first prize when, after singing the songs he had prepared, he refused to sing on sight something he didn't know. Joyce would only compete on his own terms.

That the teenage Joyce had absorbed his father's expectations and the praise of his Jesuit teachers is evident from the confident precociousness of his first literary productions. Written in 1900, aged 18, a first play was entitled *A Brilliant Career* and opened with the dedication:

> To
> My own Soul I
> Dedicate the first
> true work of my
> life.
> (Bowker, 75)

In 1902, departing on a first trip to Paris, James told his brother and confidant Stanislaus that should he die during the trip, his poetry and prose "epiphanies" must be sent to all the great libraries of the world, including the Vatican. "Remember your epiphanies," Stephen smiles to himself in *Ulysses* "written on green oval leaves, deeply deep, copies to be sent if you died to all the great libraries of the world, including Alexandria?" And he admits he has not moved on very far: "When one reads these strange pages of one long gone one feels that one is at one with one who once…"[2] The playful repetition of "one" gives a feeling of amused mastery to the admission.

As his family sank into poverty, Joyce, as yet a complete nobody, began contacting major figures in the literary world—Ibsen, George Russell, W. B. Yeats, and Lady Augusta Gregory among others—presenting himself so confidently as to risk antagonizing the people whose help he sought. Aged 19, he wrote a long letter to Ibsen to celebrate his 73rd birthday; the letter closed with the idea that the great playwright had "only opened the way" and that "higher and holier enlightenment lies—onward" (Ellmann, 87), with the young Joyce. Ibsen did not reply. A year later, having gone to great efforts to arrange an interview with Yeats, at this time the most prominent of Irish poets, Joyce spent most of the conversation criticizing the older writer, remarking on leaving that, "We have met too late. You are too old for me to have any effect on you" (Bowker, 89). Yeats was 37.

Did Joyce want to be helped, or to feel he had been let down? Or possibly both?

As he began to write, the same pattern of seeking prominence and courting rejection continued. First there were a series of quite ferocious articles directed at the Dublin literati, then endless arguments with editors about what was publishable and what wasn't. Looking ahead, none of Joyce's major works of fiction—*Dubliners, A Portrait, Ulysses, Finnegans Wake*—would be completed before being offered for publication. Each had first chapters, or sections, submitted and published at early stages of writing, and all these early publications ran into trouble with editors or censors, either for their avant-garde manner or supposedly obscene content. The effect on Joyce was never to back off or compromise as the book developed, but to raise the stakes and push the difficulty, the offence, to the limit. For this artistic integrity he has been much praised; yet, as we've seen, the habit of exasperation was standard in all Joyce's relationships.

If there is an evident escalation of "difficulty" (for publishers, censors, and readers alike) within each of the works taken singly, there is an even more marked leap between one work and the next. Each book Joyce wrote was more difficult and, for his times, more "offensive" than the last, both in general and in particular. Meantime, friends, acquaintances, and family would all recognize themselves in his pages, often disparaged, often accused of betrayal. Each book challenged everyone's loyalty to the limit, and set Joyce further and further apart.

These reflections inevitably bring us to the question: why did Joyce transform this desire for detachment, or at least a personal space where *he* called the shots, into geographical reality, "exile" as he liked to call it? Why did he leave Ireland, then stay away from Ireland, while nevertheless always writing about Ireland, and how did the fact that he lived almost all his adult life abroad at a time when communication was nothing like it is today affect his writing?

As *A Portrait* and consequent legend would have it, the young Joyce needed to go abroad to develop his writing and escape the competing demands of Catholicism and republicanism. "Living in Ireland had lost all meaning for Joyce," the biographer Gordon Bowker tells us (130). In fact before departure the young author had already completed a slim volume of poems, published two of the stories that were to make up *Dubliners*, and was getting on with his novel *Stephen Hero* with the enthusiastic but attentive criticism of Stanislaus. He had also published reviews and was showing a rare talent for provoking ire and admiration with his satires of the local literati.

All this at age 22. It's hard to imagine, then, that living in Ireland meant nothing to Joyce. On the contrary it was through measuring himself against others, his father, his brother, other writers, that he established his own self esteem, though we have to remember that in Joyce's vision there is always the sense that the really great person— Parnell is the shining example—is the hero who is magnificent in betrayal and defeat. Perhaps then we can think of Joyce's "exile," as he himself chose to call it, as simultaneously a declaration of specialness *and* defeat. However, reading through the sequence of events prior to Joyce's departure, it is evident that Nora's role was crucial.

Joyce's mother had died in 1903, depriving the family of its main element of stability. The following June James met Nora Barnacle. Up to this point his sexual experience had been mostly with prostitutes, who have the merit that they do not betray you, criticize your ideas, or make you wait long for satisfaction. Then in March 1904 a venereal infection obliged him to be more careful. Now Joyce meets an attractive, uneducated, sexually willing girl who has fled a severe father in Galway and is alone and unprotected, working as a chambermaid in Dublin. The legend will be love at first sight; nevertheless, Joyce was too ashamed of this scarcely literate beloved to introduce her to his intellectual, middle-class friends or to a father who had quite other aspirations for him. To be with Nora in Ireland would mean a battle with father and a drastic loss of his winning image; but how long would a girl be faithful if her man continued to treat her as a mistress rather than a partner? Eloping just five months after they met, Joyce could enjoy an intensely erotic cohabitation with Nora while presenting himself back in Dublin, sincerely no doubt, as an intellectual who simply had to escape the "rabblement" that was the Irish literary world. Ireland wasn't good enough for him. On the day of departure, Nora, who had no experience of travel, was sent ahead to board the ferry alone while Joyce enjoyed a proper sending off at the dockside from all his family and friends, who were to remain unaware of her presence. When his father found out he was furious. Three years later he wrote:

> I need not tell you how your miserable mistake affected my already well crushed feelings, but then maturer thoughts took more the form of pity than anger, when I saw a life of promise

crossed and a future that might have been brilliant blasted in one breath. (Bowker, 167)

Joyce's father uses the occasion to insinuate that his son's choice has ruined his chance of establishing the superior position he sought. He has become an object of pity. And Joyce *was* pitiable in these years. Writing was *not* easier in Europe than it had been in Dublin: especially since everything he wrote was about Dublin. From Paris to Zurich to Trieste and the remote Pola on the northern Adriatic, Joyce struggled to find work as a language teacher, struggled to survive the boredom of language teaching, struggled to find rooms to rent, struggled to pay the rent, struggled to find people who would lend him money, struggled to keep Nora, who understood nothing and knew no one, in good spirits. Communication with Ireland and publishers was slow and discouraging. Editors were willing to publish if he would compromise a little with the "obscenity" and disrespectful political opinions. He would not, if only because yielding, in the background he came from, was more or less synonymous with defeat (something made blisteringly clear in the Christmas lunch confrontation between nationalism and Catholicism in *A Portrait*). The more depressed he became, the more he spent what cash remained on drink.

Nevertheless Joyce hurried to become a paterfamilias; it was a form of assertion and a kind of success. A first child was named George after James's younger brother who had died three years before. Such was the loyalty to home. Nora fell into depression. Bent on "the spiritual liberation of [his] country," as *A Portrait* would have it, Joyce wrote to his Aunt Josephine for advice as to how to cheer her up and cheered himself up by going to prostitutes. Desperate for company, he invited Stanislaus to join them, then exploited him quite shamelessly, taking his help and language-school earnings for granted; simply, Stanislaus was at his service, an errand boy and a source of emergency income. On a whim, Joyce went to Rome, got a job in a bank, hated everything, then returned to Trieste and Stanislaus's enforced charity. A second child, Lucia, was born. Only 25, already a patriarch, Joyce's health was deteriorating, his eyesight in particular.

It was during this period, with the writing of *The Dead* in 1907, that a distinctive Joycean note is established for the first time: a powerful nostalgia for Ireland colours the prose with a sadness and sense of defeat; Joyce is not in the place that matters to him.

The action of *The Dead*, we remember, takes place in Dublin, on the last Christmas when Joyce was in Ireland. Gabriel, a young literature teacher powerfully attached to a community that he feels he has no place in, takes centre stage at a music teachers' Christmas party to give an exaggeratedly intellectual, deliberately non-nationalist speech that he knows will go over everyone's heads and irritate them. Returning home, he seeks erotic consolation with his wife only to discover she is pining for a boyfriend who died long ago, a boy who had committed to her totally and fatally, in a way he, Gabriel, cannot. Culturally and intellectually above everyone else, he is sentimentally abandoned, isolated, defeated; with no way forward, his static melancholy is transformed into a haunting vision of his whole country as a graveyard frozen to stillness under snow. The moment of greatest loneliness, loss of direction and defeat is the moment when the wholeness of the community is most beautifully and forlornly invoked and the writer's skill most powerfully affirmed. Self esteem is fused with loss; the one feeds the other: the more the Joycean hero is superior to those around him the more he is deemed irrelevant to the world he describes and suffers for it. Beneath the sadness and nostalgia, there is a feeling of betrayal: "Perhaps she had not told him all the story,"[3] he thinks of his wife.

Having now withdrawn, not merely to a corner of the room while others got on with the party, but to a corner of Europe a thousand miles from home, Joyce desperately needed to get his work published so as to have his friends back in Ireland remember that they were still in relation with him, still in competition for him. And when he was published it was important they be aware of it and worry about it. In this regard it's hard to think of a writer who put more of his friends and his acquaintances into his books, often disparagingly, often with the intention of settling scores. The brilliance of the work is a declaration of his superiority to those he attacks. On the other hand, each publication is also a lamentation of his loss of Ireland. For the reader, so long as this sense of loss and nostalgia is to the fore, one can feel close to Joyce and enjoy his lyricism, comedy, and evocation of mind in place. When, in the later work, the style seems to impose the author's winning intellect on the reader, and lyricism and comedy are harder to access, then some readers will begin to feel uncomfortable.

In 1909 Joyce returned, twice, to Ireland, once alone, once with George, now usually called Giorgio, but not with Nora. On the first of these occasions he was told that Nora had betrayed him with a friend prior to their departure from Dublin and in response wrote her hysterical letters of accusation. They show Joyce's readiness to feel betrayed and his intense fear of the loss of personal prestige he believed was involved. Later, persuaded that the story of Nora's unfaithfulness was a lie (hence an act of treachery by his enemies rather than by her, hence something that made him more important, in so far as others needed to attack him), he first wrote to her asking forgiveness for the earlier letters, then again, fantasizing a ferocious eroticism; "I wish to be lord of your body and soul," he announced (Bowker, 182). A situation had developed where life with Nora was essential, but only possible far away from Ireland where she was unhappy and work difficult, and only acceptable if he had complete control, something Nora never granted. Nora would never, for example, acknowledge that she liked or even read his books. To keep her company in the trap they had fallen into, Joyce brought back to Trieste two younger Joyce sisters from Dublin, first Eva then Eileen. Later they would all be joined, at some expense for shipping, by the Joyce family portraits as the author pursued his reconstruction of Dublin away from Dublin with himself as head of the community.

Before going on to consider the moment when Joyce's publishing fortunes begin to change, how can we see him in light of Ugazio's ideas on personality and semantic polarities? Courage and independence were important for him, but he never seemed to have thought twice about these matters. He was courageous to the point of rashness and supremely independent. Although his characters may often be afraid, fear is never the defining emotion in his work. Good and evil are present in the books in abundance, but as a manifestation of a Catholic culture which Joyce and his alter egos seek to escape and outgrow. There is no question in the life or the work of "agenbite of inwit" (the prick of conscience Stephen Dedalus fears) as anything more than a nod to a rather crude mental trap that others are setting for him.

The question of belonging is more complex. Joyce remains absolutely attached to Ireland, despite all his years away, yet simultaneously feels that Ireland is beneath him, its culture inferior. Rather than
concern about exclusion from the community, he is worried that his
undying attachment to it will diminish him, that he may be circumscribed by it. Yet looking at the novels, aside from the alter ego's with-
drawals from the community into superior isolation, there is not much
talk about being in and out, included and excluded, the kind of
vocabulary that saturates Dickens's writing, and Woolf's. Rather, his
position is that of one who turns his "exile" into a weapon against
those who still form his mental community. In fact it is when we consider issues of winning and losing, of constant confrontation, that we
feel this is central to everything Joyce writes and does. Ugazio remarks:

> The *conflict over the definition of the relationship is a continual issue in the
> conversation of these families*. The subject matter being argued
> over—the "contents" of the conflict—is generally irrelevant:
> what is important is supremacy (one-upmanship), so that inter-
> actions are dominated by symmetrical hubris. (Ugazio, 185)

Reading this observation, it is hard not to think of the extraordinary
Christmas lunch in *A Portrait*, where various relatives become involved
in a ferocious argument over the Catholic Church's role in the downfall of Parnell. It is the intransigence of all the parties that is remarkable, to the point that the discussion itself seems less important
than the brutal confrontation of will between the various members.
Stephen's mother is the only member ready to compromise, if only in
order to have the argument end, but she comes off as the loser, while
her relationship with her husband shifts ominously between her simply ordering him to stop arguing and behave, which he sheepishly
agrees to do, then his ferociously returning to the argument and winding it up, leaving her defeated rather than dominant. Alongside the
battle between the nationalist and Catholic contingents, that is, there
is a second battle between husband and wife over the nature of their
relationship. This battle remains just as unresolved as the louder battle
over Parnell.

Stephen, needless to say, is absolutely neutral as to the issues at stake
at the Christmas lunch, which at his age he doesn't understand. For him

this is simply a conflict of personalities, an exercise in bloody-minded rivalry. Earlier, at college he had reflected on these arguments thus:

> He wondered if they were arguing at home about that. That was called politics. There were two sides in it: Dante was on one side and his father and Mr Casey were on the other side but his mother and uncle Charles were on no side. (chapter 1)

Throughout the dramatic argument over lunch, which is character-ized by a powerful sense of entrapment, as none of those involved seems able to find a way out of total warfare, Stephen concentrates on observing the combatants' physical tics and their particular ways of speaking, the sounds of the words. In this way he detaches himself from the argument, so that we might imagine he is freeing himself from the unhappy dynamic that is tearing his family apart. Later we appreciate that precisely the refusal to engage in the argument becomes a new way of seeking to gain the upper hand, for although Stephen will reject the nationalist/Catholic conflict, he cannot escape this habit of measuring himself against the others. As we have said, as soon as Joyce started writing, the first published items from his pen had been ferociously polemical articles aimed at other writers *because* they were taking sides in the nationalist debate. He hasn't withdrawn from the battle but shifted the battleground. His detachment from the immediate discussion opens the possibility of opposing *everyone* from his own separate position; in "The Holy Office," one of the earliest satires, he describes himself as "a stag at bay" flashing "my antlers on the air" (Bowker, 127).

It was while Joyce was writing *A Portrait*, in 1913, that Ezra Pound entered his life and everything changed. In his role as intellectual scout seeking "markedly modern stuff" (Bowker, 210), Pound singled out Joyce as one of the most innovative writers of his time and helped him to start publishing in the literary review, *The Egoist*, a paper look-ing to satisfy the growing demand, in part from the academic commu-nity, for more cerebral and experimental poetry and fiction. Pound would now be Joyce's fervent disciple and unflagging promoter for many years. In a sense, you might say Pound's commitment presented a new challenge for Joyce: how would it ever be possible to ask too much of this man, or indeed of the literary professors whose taste he was feeding and directing? It seemed Pound was willing to do everything for him.

Joyce's fortunes now began to swing from failure to success. The first chapter of *A Portrait* was published in *The Egoist* in 1914. *Dubliners* was also published the same year. *Exiles* had already been finished. *Ulysses* was well under way. It was the moment of breakthrough. However, if you have an enduring image of yourself as a stag at bay, an image that aligns you with the betrayed Parnell, and perhaps too with your exhausted and drunken father, then success may be more disorienting than struggle and failure. Or we could say that Joyce had got used to the portrayal of himself as a struggling hero, and that this image had become an integral part of the success of what he had written, one man against everybody.

In this scenario it may well be that the only thing such a person can do with success is to use it as a stepping stone to further calamity. Rather than calming down as things got better, Joyce continued to ask far more than was reasonable of Stanislaus and Nora and to make unusual demands of his publishers (typically Joyce would demand that a book be published on his birthday, or the anniversary of the day he met Nora, then would overwhelm the publisher with last-minute proof corrections). Taking the family to neutral Zurich when the First World War broke out, he received financial support from the Royal Literary Fund and the British Treasury Fund. This was very much thanks to Pound's lobbying. Joyce promptly did what he could to drink this money away, then spoiled his relationship with the British authorities by engaging in a futile argument with a consulate employee, Henry Carr, over a small sum of money that Carr believed he was owed when Joyce staged a play using English-speaking actors. Very soon his funding was discontinued. Again Pound solved the situation, introducing Joyce to Harriet Weaver, editor of *The Egoist* and wealthy heiress. In 1917 she undertook to maintain Joyce economically so that his genius could flourish. Apparently she was offering a blank cheque. Again Joyce squandered much of what she sent him on smart restaurants, expensive hotels, magnanimous tips, and drink.

Having described his fellow citizens in *Dubliners* as morally bankrupt, bigoted, beaten, and occasionally paedophile, having presented Irish society in *A Portrait* as suffocating under the competing demands of nationalism and Catholicism, Joyce wrote *Exiles*, a play that few have read and fewer have seen. It presents an impasse of extreme complexity between four characters: a couple who resemble Joyce and Nora in every way (she not educated enough to understand his brilliant writing, etc.) and a pair of their friends, who are both cousins and ex-lovers (between themselves); of the two friends, the man, who is the Joyce figure's best friend, but also a writerly rival, is eager to become the Nora figure's lover, while the woman, who is intellectual and romantic, is courted (romantically and intellectually) by the Joyce figure. Unlike the others in this unhappy love rectangle, the Joyce figure knows of the relationship between his wife and friend, but does not intervene. On the contrary he observes, perhaps even instigates. Then, to the wife's great embarrassment, he tells his friend that he knows of their relationship, but again without intervening, suggesting that they become lovers, if that's what they want. He also tells his friend of his interest in his cousin/ex-lover, but without acting on this interest. Totally involved in the group, he nevertheless seems to be inviting the others to decide whether to do without him or not, transforming their betrayal into a position of power. Presented as openness, honesty, and generosity on the Joyce figure's part (his willingness to let them do as they wish), this uneasy stance actually intensifies the impasse between the four, who end the play in an agony of uncertainty, none of them sure of the nature of any of the relationships they have with the other three and hence increasingly unclear about their own identities.

Very much in the manner of Ibsen, the style and language of *Exiles* is as simple as the plot is convoluted and perverse. Needless to say, there were problems of propriety and obscenity. Completed in 1915, it would not be shown on stage in English until 1925 and never convinced either public or critics. The one time, that is, that Joyce sought to present the core of his sentimental life (for the facts behind the plot are well documented) without any embellishment, he had failed. At which point we may note that it is never Joyce's plots that interest readers in the more celebrated works. Meantime, the writing of *Exiles* pushed Nora's loyalty to the limit, in that the public were more or less invited to identify the protagonists with Joyce and Nora. The play itself was part of a real life story, similar to the story it describes.

In *Ulysses*, which was written during the years when Joyce was trying to find a producer for *Exiles*, Bloom, one of the book's two Joycean alter egos, does not intervene to prevent his wife from betraying him, while Stephen, the other alter ego, does not resolve his difficult relationship with his father. More impasse, more melancholy uncertainty surrounding intimate relationships. In compensation, however, and in complete contrast to *Exiles*, we now have a host of mythical parallels, puns, extravagant examples of pastiche and experimentalism that, page after page, submerge the plot in an ocean of encyclopaedic prose as lively as it is bizarre. The unhappy relationships remain a source of pain, but the attention is constantly shifted elsewhere in a process that allows the author to show off all his stylistic genius and present himself, the writer, as very much a winner; or rather, Joyce is as much a winner as an artist as his alter egos are, in many senses, losers in life. It's also true that while *Dubliners* and *A Portrait* might still, here and there, be mistaken for more traditional literature, this was no longer possible with *Ulysses*. From now on Joyce had to be thought of as outside the pack, in a space of his own creation. But not cut loose. Rather this space was opposed to the conventional space, doing battle with it, looking back to it as it looks back to Dublin.

The novel opens with intense sparring and rivalry between Stephen, Buck Mulligan, and their English acquaintance Haines, Stephen in particular being constantly concerned with power relations and prestige. Even to carry out a small service for Buck, lend him a handkerchief, lend him some money, is to lay himself open to the depressing consideration that he is "serving." A loan bolsters the self esteem of the borrower who has the power to command it, not the lender whose arm is twisted into giving it, an attitude predicated on the assumption that as a rule loans won't be paid back, or only when the lender chooses to pay. Irish art is "the cracked looking glass of a servant" (*Ulysses*, 13), hierarchically subject to England, but to have thought of such a clever aphorism brings a welcome feeling of superiority, especially if the idea can be turned into money by selling it to Haines, though again this reminds Stephen of the Englishman's superior wealth. When the woman bringing the three young men their milk for breakfast asks Buck if he is a medical student, Stephen is scornful: "She bows her old head to a voice that speaks to her loudly, her bonesetter, her medicineman; me she slights" (*Ulysses*, 20).

About Joyce it is common to say that his prose shifts constantly, is never at rest, the syntax always uneasy;[4] it would make sense, I think, to refer this to the way Joyce's alter egos are endlessly measuring their status against that of whoever they are with. It's hard in this first chapter, for example, not to feel that Stephen is desperately insecure as he constantly looks for ways in which other people may be diminishing him. The fascination with language and his mastery of it is always used as a weapon to fight back.

In the following chapters we find Bloom moving in the same world of values, but occupying a position that is complementary to Stephen's. I should say at once here that while on my three or four readings of *Ulysses* I have never had any problem believing in Stephen, Bloom was initially a mystery to me, a figure I simply couldn't believe in or engage with, and this is strange of course, for Bloom is frequently presented by enthusiastic critics as the first "all-round man" in fiction, the first character who, to be blunt, eats, digests, pisses, shits, masturbates, etc. In fact, we could say that the core of *Ulysses* remained for many years a huge enigmatic episode, for me. In this sense: we meet Bloom on the day his wife is going to betray him with a concert impresario and he is aware of this; what I would then expect—and we shall discuss where I am coming from and why I would expect this in a later chapter—is that he, Bloom, would think constantly about this betrayal, try to determine how to react, be anguished about his inability to confront his wife, etc. I would not expect him to get on with his day thinking about a million other things, showing himself to be extremely affable and in general contributing to the encyclopaedic vocation of Joyce's book. As a result it always seemed to me that Joyce was more interested in the encyclopaedic aspect of the work, in his modernist creation, his fine and clever descriptions, than a credible presentation of Bloom's psychology, a credible *drama*. In contrast to Stephen, he seems unbelievably laid back.

Jung, who was invited to write a preface of *Ulysses* for the German edition, puts this and other elements in the novel down to a strategy of evasion similar to that of schizophrenics. In order not to confront the stalled relationship with Molly, Bloom thinks about more or less everything under the sun, giving extraordinary attention and care to matters physical and practical, and all this in a language of lyrical gentleness that, as it were, removes the sting of an event that cannot be faced; Jung assumes this is also Joyce's own strategy in not dealing with issues in the author's own life, issues more openly confronted in *Exiles*.

Jung's idea of evasion makes some sense and might to a certain extent be validated by Joyce himself who referred to his later style in *Finnegans Wake* as "the JJ safety pun factory" (Bowker, 360)—the puns draw attention away from the book's unhappy content, avoiding a transparency that would be painful. However, talk of the strategy of the schizophrenic is hardly convincing in *Ulysses*, since Bloom seems anything but challenged in his mental health. On the contrary, he comes across as the book's kindest and nicest figure, the novel's charmer. And though it's true that Bloom spends much of his day thinking about other things, Molly is never far from his mind, nor does he live in denial about what is going on.

As I say, there were times when this anomaly, for me—Bloom's seeming equanimity—disqualified Joyce's book as dramatic narrative, leaving it largely a compendium of Dublin and an exercise in experimental modernism with more of a symbolic structure than a credible story. However, when one begins to think of Joyce's characters in terms of the position they occupy in this winner/loser polarity, then a number of things become clear. Where Stephen won't serve, Bloom serves everyone. As we open the book he feeds his cat, he takes tea to his wife in bed, he shops for the family, later he attends a funeral, he plans how to assist the dead man's widow, he keeps away from home to allow his wife to betray him in peace. Above all, he comes to Stephen's assistance, offering him the protection he has lost with the death of his mother, associating him with his own son who died shortly after birth, never competing with the boy but accommodating him. Stephen, on the other hand, hardly gives his protector much satisfaction and refuses his offer to stay the night, much as he refused to bow to his mother's will. Sexually, Bloom is in secret correspondence with a woman with a view to a possible affair that seems unlikely ever to happen, masturbates at the seashore spying a crippled girl's knickers, flirts in a brothel but doesn't actually have sex.

Bloom, then, is in many ways a loser. He never has the upper hand. Ugazio remarks:

> As well as the "winner/loser" polarity, these families also have a second polarity—"strong-willed/yielding"—which is hierarchically dependent on the first, based on a relation of means to an end. These people are winners because they are wilful,

determined or efficient, or they are losers because they are passive, compliant or liable to give in to others. Affability, amena-bility, acceptance of the definition given by the other person to the relationship are construed within these families as passivity, faint-heartedness, ineptitude. (Ugazio, 182)

Turning to the first episode that presents Bloom, we at once have the same mechanism we saw with Stephen of comparing oneself with others and imagining how the other sees us; only this time, the "other" is the cat. "Wonder what I look like to her," Bloom thinks. "Height of a tower? No, she can jump me" (*Ulysses*, 57). When he arrives in his wife's bedroom after a visit to the butcher's to buy kidneys, he is brusquely henpecked. Everything she says suggests impatience on her part and incompetence on his, whereas in fact Bloom has been taking immense care to do everything "right" for her, "righting her breakfast things on the humpy tray . . . Another slice of bread and butter: three, four: right. She didn't like her plate full. Right" (*Ulysses*, 57), so that we suspect he finds pleasure in competence, though partly because of his anxiety that she will criticize him if he makes a mistake. In her room he brings her the post, including, as he knows, a letter from her lover; he raises the blinds at her request, he clears her clothes from a chair, he acknowledges her imperatives about hurrying with the tea and scald-ing the teapot, he doesn't complain when she complains about his slowness, he straightens the bedspread, he offers to open the window, he fishes the cheap novel he has bought her from behind the bed where she has let it drop.

In short, Bloom allows himself to be entirely dominated, and is always gentle in his service. Entering the logic of the dynamic Joyce's characters seem to share, he enjoys the relief involved in *not* seeking in any way to be on top, of not struggling against another's demands, but rather serving them in every way, with generosity; or we might say, the relief of being so in love that service is possible without a collapse of self esteem.

Yet, despite his acknowledgement of defeat in certain aspects of life, we always feel Bloom is confident of his intellectual superiority, which eventually emerges when his wife asks him what the word "metempsychosis" means. He warms to his explanation and comes at it in various ways; hardly listening, she warns him that he is burning something in the kitchen, the kidneys, and thus reasserts her dominance in the practical sphere. But Bloom is safe in his mental world. On the lavatory he "envied kindly" (what a collocation!) the writer of the prize-winning story in *Titbits* who has made £3 13s 6d from his story. When he wipes himself with the page the story is published on, it is without the resentment or the sense of vendetta Stephen might have felt. But he does wipe himself with the story; he is not in awe of any writer.

To conclude, however unappealing it might be to live with a woman who is betraying you, Bloom appears to have found a mental balance that allows him to handle the situation, or, if we want to see this negatively, that allows the problematic relationship to become chronic. Part of his strategy will involve being physically away from home all day, and mentally always moving off at tangents, generating much of the book's extraordinary proliferation.

This brings us to a consideration that I believe is crucial when reading Joyce. As we've said the author is forever presenting us with an immediate situation, where the protagonist risks being a loser, in reaction to which he creates a mental elsewhere where he is a winner. We might say then that in Joyce's own life, *the style he developed is the elsewhere he is creating.* He writes in English, but more and more it is *his* English. He writes about Ireland, but deeper reality is with Europe and myth. The work is not only an elsewhere, but claiming superiority to the standard somewhere. Meaning is not at home, with a wife who may or more likely may not be faithful, but with Odysseus who wanders abroad. However, the sense of loss in not being able to be in Ireland, not being successful *at home*, is never healed and is intensely felt to be someone else's fault.

To read Joyce is to be drawn toward this way of thinking about the world, invited to attribute greater importance to the intellectual and aesthetic life where we (Joyce and the reader) are highly competent, than to the world of immediate relationships and drama, where we risk losing. The attractions of this formula to the cloistered academic will be evident, a thought that prompts this reflection: that almost all literary criticism is written by the kind of person who chooses to become a cloistered academic; perhaps if written by other equally intelligent people the burden of literary criticism would be quite different. But these other "equally intelligent" people have no reason for writing literary criticism.

For those readers who had responded positively to Joyce's earlier works, accepting things that seemed iffy and challenging in return for the discovery of a fine new writer, the appearance of *Ulysses* raised the stakes enormously. Aside from the sheer scope and strenuousness of the text, there was a more provocative level of obscenity, in particular the scene where Bloom masturbates, sneaking glances at the young Gerty MacDowell's panties as she leans back from the parapet she is sitting on to follow the rockets of a firework display. This porn-pamphlet material was to be redeemed by the brilliance of the writing, in this case a lavishly ironic pastiche of magazines for young women. The same was true of the long episode in a brothel. The freshness and experimentalism of the approach, Joyce's mastery of every possible style of English, must make the evident excitement in writing about sex and prostitutes acceptable.

It didn't work for everyone. Stanislaus, Joyce's favourite brother and hitherto most assiduous helper, described the brothel episode as "the most horrible thing in literature" nothing more than an "inspection of the stinkpots" (Bowker, 303). The novel was banned in both England and the States. There was a battle over what could and what could not be put in a book.

It goes without saying that Joyce read reviews avidly, since this was the moment to measure himself against others. He rarely minded criticism or denunciations of scandal; what mattered was to be at the centre of debate. Others would not always concede your genius because they were envious, but they would envy your being the talk of the town. One example will do for all in this. When Jung completed the essay he had been asked to write as a preface to the German edition of *Ulysses*, it was scathing:

> The whole work has the character of a worm cut in half, that can grow a new head or a new tail as required...This singular and uncanny characteristic of the Joycean mind shows that his work pertains to the class of cold-blooded animals and specifically to the worm family. If worms were gifted with literary powers they would write with the sympathetic nervous system for lack of a brain. I suspect that something of this kind has happened to Joyce, that here we have a case of visceral thinking with severe restrictions of cerebral activity and its confinement to the perceptual processes.[5]

Despite the insulting tone, Joyce asked the publishers *to use the piece anyway*; he felt confident that, measuring Jung against himself, people would feel he came out the winner. His publishers decided not to take the risk.

Joyce's own most famous comment on *Ulysses* was that he had "put in so many enigmas and puzzles, it'll keep the professors busy for centuries" (Bowker, 7). The remark establishes a direct hierarchy where the professors serve Joyce by running semantic errands from one part of the text to another, or from *Ulysses* to *The Odyssey* and back. It also suggests the inspiration behind Joyce's next project. Aware that his masterpiece had divided critics between those who praised it generously, using it to bolster their agendas for experimental fiction, and those who thought its obscurity and obscenity had gone too far, Joyce now settled down to put the loyalty of his supporters to the supreme test with a work whose title he wouldn't reveal until its publication eighteen years later.

The plot of *Finnegans Wake* cannot confidently be summarized; I'll just say that a father is accused of sexual crimes, which, though never made specific, apparently include incest, while his wife asks their son and writer (a man with weak eyesight) to write a letter defending the father. Though much talked about, the letter does not appear in the book. For his part Joyce claimed that the novel amounted to a history of the world from its origins to the twentieth century. But it is hardly the plot people notice on tackling *Finnegans Wake*; for the style, indeed the language, now constitutes a far more radical "elsewhere" than had the prose of *Ulysses*. Essentially, while *Ulysses* created its effects to a large degree through the idiosyncratic ordering of words in the sentence ("perfume of embraces all him assailed," 168), in *Finnegans Wake* a high proportion of the words are portmanteaux, often made up with elements from various languages ("And thanacestross mound have swollup them all," 18). Here are a few lines:

> Snip snap snoody. Noo err historyend goody. Of a lil trip trap and a big treeskooner for he put off the ketyl and they made three (for fie!) and if hec dont love alpy then lad you annoy me. For hanigen with hunigen still haunt ahunt to finnd their hinnigen where Pappappapparrassannuaragheallachnatullaghmonganmacmacmacwhackfalltherdebblenonthedubblandadd—ydoodled and anruly person creeked a jest. Gestapose to parry

off cheekars or frankfurters on the odor. Fine again, Cuoholson! Peace, O wiley! (*Finnegans*, 332)

On the one hand it might appear that Joyce has now detached himself entirely from the conventional literary community. On the other you could say that he is trapped in an escalating schismogenesis of the kind described by Bateson in *Naven*: the more that worried editors or unhappy readers insist on propriety and comprehensibility, the more Joyce gives them impropriety and incomprehensibility. To the extent, then, that *Finnegans Wake* is a logical escalation from *Ulysses*, Joyce's supporters should have been happy. On the other hand, one might also speak of a threshold's having been passed and a law of diminishing returns kicking in. Joyce was inviting readers through a looking glass into a Wonderland where, like the Red Queen, only he knew the rules and only he could play. In the event the first pages of the *Wake* succeeded in exasperating Pound and Weaver, both of them finding it incomprehensible and unappealing. Joyce's brother Stanislaus accused him of wanting "to show that you are a superclever superman with a super style" and of "competing with Miss [Gertrude] Stein" (Bowker, 413). It's interesting that it is his brother who perceives the competitive element. They grew up in the same environment. Depressed and inflamed by such treachery, Joyce made the book more complex; if, when reading it to friends, he found they understood too easily, he revised it to raise the bar. Really to be superior was to be beyond the understanding of the ordinary man. Though this would make Joyce a loser economically, it would be a glorious defeat.

One says of Joyce that he lived in Paris in these years between the publication of *Ulysses* in 1922 and *Finnegans Wake* in 1939. In fact he rarely stayed more than a few months in the same place, enjoying weeks at a time in luxury hotels in many parts of France, Belgium, and Switzerland with frequent trips to England and even an attempt to set up home in London. Endless eyesight problems increased his already remarkable capacity to get people to do things for him. The young Beckett felt he exaggerated them to seem more vulnerable.

Despite frequent stomach pains, stress-related he believed, Joyce continued to drink heavily. His steady income now suspended with Harriet Weaver's desertion, he nevertheless refused to do any writing for money. "The only writing for money I ever do is to you" (Bowker, 438), he told Weaver. He would not use his pen in any public debate or engage with society in any way. Nor would he offer any preface, or explanation to his *Work in Progress*, something that the literary journals would have been glad to pay for. There must be no mediation.

Meantime, Joyce's relationship with Nora was now in serious stalemate with both parties argumentative and unsatisfied. In this regard it's worth remembering Nora's response to the famous monologue by Bloom's wife that closes *Ulysses*. In so far as Molly Bloom was understood to be based on Nora (something Joyce had made clear), the monologue is easily construed as Joyce seeing himself through his wife's eyes, and hence seeking to define their relationship, ultimately on a positive note as Molly says yes to her life and her man. Nora wouldn't let him have this victory. Whenever the monologue was talked about she bluntly remarked: "He knows nothing at all about women" (Bowker, 441).

The couple did define their relationship in legal terms in 1931, marrying after twenty-six years of cohabitation, mainly to clarify questions of inheritance, but this did not resolve the unease between them. Nora was now constantly threatening to leave if her husband didn't change his ways—the drinking and overspending—but always staying despite his refusal to do so. Then, in 1932, the couple's daughter Lucia showed her mother how one might stop the great Joyce from always doing exactly what he wanted: as she and her parents prepared to board the boat train to London at Gare du Nord for a trip that Lucia did not want to make, she threw a fit so violent that Joyce was forced to stay in Paris. It was the first of many psychotic episodes, many of which seemed to be, as it were, aimed at her father.

Some biographers have hinted that the adolescent Lucia was possibly the object of her father's sexual attentions, but this seems the merest hearsay. When we hear Lucia herself speak, in letters or reported conversations, the bitterness is all for Joyce's monomania, his always occupying the centre of attention and his wasting the money that might have been his children's inheritance. On one visit to friends Lucia threatened to leave if anyone so much as mentioned her father. On another we find her insisting to one of Joyce's admirers and helpers that "her father was a failure and a physical wreck who could neither write nor sleep on account of a ruined constitution" (Bowker, 339). In short, a loser.

Such was the rivalry in the family for Joyce's attention that no sooner had Lucia moved centre stage with the psychotic episode at the railway station, than both Nora and above all Giorgio (recently married to a wealthy American divorcée ten years his senior) were calling for her to be committed to a mental hospital. Lucia countered, but also in a sense helped her antagonists, by attacking her mother and twice setting fire to her room. Torn between his writing, his elsewhere where he was all powerful, and the appalled recognition that something real, terrible, and possibly irreversible was taking place in the here and now—a drama of the kind he would never tackle openly in his writing—Joyce wavered, allowed Lucia to be committed then fetched her back, then allowed her to be committed again, and so on. At this point when he and Nora took their expensive holidays away from Paris he arranged for postcards to be sent to Lucia from back in town as if he were still at home, a stratagem that feels like something from the pages of *Ulysses*, or indeed Simenon's Maigret, and of course required asking others to run confidential errands for him. Joyce appears to have understood the changes Lucia was demanding he make, but once she was committed to the mental hospital there was no need for him to make them. Meantime, in care she became a huge drain on the financial resources she had complained he was squandering.

In 1936 a Danish writer, Ole Vinding, met Joyce in Copenhagen and quoted him as admitting: "Since 1922 my book has become more real to me than reality...all other things have been insurmountable difficulties." "He sucked energy from his surroundings," Vinding observed, and of the relationship with Nora remarked, "[Joyce] was like a spoiled boy with his quiet, eternally permissive mother" (Bowker, 452).

Finnegans Wake was eventually finished in 1938 and published in 1939, again after much wrangling with publishers about significant dates. Joyce seemed finished with it. "We're going downhill fast" (Bowker, 516), Beckett reports him having said with some satisfaction as he and Nora left Paris for Zurich to escape the Nazi advance; as if, having completed the world where he was victorious, he might as well consummate his defeat in the real world as soon as possible. Some four weeks after crossing the border into Switzerland, the author was taken ill and died in a matter of days with a perforated bowel.

Meantime *Finnegans Wake* divided even the most competent readers. Writers as different as H. G. Wells, D. H. Lawrence, Cesare Pavese, and Vladimir Nabokov all came out strongly against the book. Jacques Derrida, Northrop Frye, and later Anthony Burgess and Harold Bloom were all very much in favour. There is little middle ground in this debate. But it is the terms of the dismissal or the acclaim that are interesting, for they suggest how readers have been drawn into the Joycean win/lose semantic. Some reject the book as a scandalous demand on their time and take pleasure in rejecting Joyce's bid for superiority; others not only praise it but happily make explicit their sense of awed submission.

Here is Wells in a personal letter to the author:

> you have turned your back on common men, on their elemen-
> tary needs and their restricted time and intelligence ... I ask: who
> the hell is this Joyce who demands so many waking hours of the
> few thousands I have still to live for a proper appreciation of his
> quirks and fancies and flashes of rendering? (Ellmann, 688)

Thornton Wilder on the contrary loves solving Joyce's puzzles:

> one of my absorptions ... has been James Joyce's new novel, dig-
> ging out its buried keys and resolving that unbroken chain of
> erudite puzzles and finally coming on lots of wit, and lots of
> beautiful things has been my midnight recuperation. A lot
> of thanks to him.[6]

Beside these fixed positions, and rather more interestingly, there are many people who *radically change their position* in relation to Joyce's work, suggesting that this business of measuring oneself against the author, a habit Joyce encourages, is something that has to be thought out again and again. It as if the extravagance of style, combined with a lack of narrative tension or focused content, continually obliges the reader to raise the question, is this good or isn't it, is it or isn't it a waste of time? And the need to keep asking that question encourages us to keep coming back to the books.

Louis Gillet, a French editor and critic, was a classic example; after writing a highly critical review of *Ulysses* describing it as "indigestible" and "meaningless" (Bowker, 345), he then made a complete U-turn expressing his "humility and devotion" (Bowker, 410) to Joyce and went on to write a highly positive review of what was then *Work in Progress*, admiring its superimposed meanings, unities and universes, musicality, and so on. About actual content little was said, something disconcertingly frequent in responses to Joyce; one applauds the performance, without much comment on substance. Or perhaps the subject *is* the performance. In this regard, it's intriguing how hearing Joyce's work read out loud, preferably by the author himself, but if not by a good actor, is often the turning point for many who follow Gillet's conversion. The reading voice offers the mediation, the explanation, the *justification*, that Joyce would never offer *in the text*. A reviewer in the *New English Weekly* suggested reading *Finnegans Wake* aloud "with an empty mind... impersonally." This way "the full beauty of the rhythm and the peculiar turn of the words becomes apparent" (Bowker, 388). Again no mention of content. Curiously, Joyce himself liked to have others read his work aloud to him, something I have not heard of any other author enjoying.

Samuel Beckett's Joycean journey went the other way from Gillet's: he first admires *Work in Progress*, because it pushes English, a language "abstracted to death," radically close to experience—"when the subject is dance the words dance, when the subject is sleep the words go to sleep."[7] This was the phase when the young Beckett ran errands for Joyce, took dictation for him, even copied his mannerisms. But not long afterwards Beckett realizes that this influence and subjugation may be dangerous to him. He complains that his own writing "stinks of Joyce" (Bowker, 384). He observes Joyce's tendency to assume a position of omnipotence and omniscience and decides that the older writer's belief that words can "say anything you want them to if only you put them in the right order" is ingenuous. "I swear that I will go beyond JJ before I die,"[8] he says in 1932, recognizing he has entered into a kind of competition, a challenge he doesn't want to accept. And he begins to speak positively of failure, of the reality of impotence as over against the illusion of eloquent control. If Joyce was victorious in his evocation of the world of sense and perception, Beckett would "fail," but "fail better,"[9] a complex act of positioning within the winner/loser polarity. In the end, he concludes, the evocative capacity that Joyce had mastered was misleading because the word is inevitably and always distant from experience and impotent to express it, so that to use language is always to experience failure. So Beckett arrives at a position now diametrically opposed to Joyce: using language for Joyce is winning; using language for Becket is losing. Losing, or failing better, means having the impotence of language emerge, not hiding it and pretending otherwise.

But perhaps the most revealing rereading of *Ulysses* is Jung's. We've seen how insulting Jung's first reaction was. That was in 1930. The book "refused to meet him half way," he said. It gave "the reader an irritating sense of inferiority." Its "incredible versatility of style" paradoxically "has a monotonous and hypnotic effect,"[10] it is bereft of any real sentiment, hence the kind of thing only aesthetes would like, and so on. Two years later, however, Jung modified his essay, sent it to Joyce and in a cover letter confessed that he had been unable to leave the book alone. "Your *Ulysses* has presented the world such an upsetting psychological problem that repeatedly I have been called in as a supposed authority on psychological matters" (Ellmann, 629).

At once we see Jung measuring himself up against Joyce. Joyce has set the problem, and so is an important person. But Jung is the authority. He goes on to say what an exceedingly "hard nut" *Ulysses* has proved. He has mulled over it for three years. Nevertheless he is grateful because "I learned a great deal from it" (Ellmann, 629). Though he is not sure whether he actually enjoyed it. He cursed and he admired. In the new version of the essay attached to the letter he redeems *Ulysses* by suggesting that, *unbeknown to its author*, its constant erosion of sentiment and engagement, its determined evasion and detachment, its "moon-like" vision of the world, has the function of arriving at a mental state similar to Buddhist detachment, a perception of the vanity of any involvement in the world.

> Joyce's inexpressibly rich and myriad-faceted language unfolds itself in passages that creep along tapeworm fashion, terribly boring and monotonous, but the very boredom and monotony of it attain an epic grandeur that makes the book a "Mahabharata" of the world's futility and squalor. (Jung, 128)

The comedy of the situation is obvious: Jung begins to feel positive about the book when he can give it a sense that even its author didn't realize it has. He has gone beyond Joyce. He is thus superior to those who simply turn away from the book *and* from those who go on its knees to its author.

Jung could easily have published his essay without writing to Joyce personally, but is drawn to do so because the letter gives him a chance to define his relationship with Joyce directly, in his favour of course. Joyce reacts in line with what we have come to expect, rejecting this definition, declaring Jung (in a letter to his publisher) an "imbecile" (Ellmann, 629), but at the same time feeling flattered that so much attention has been given him by such a famous man. What matters for our purposes is that his book has created among its readers precisely the kind of competitive, hierarchizing dynamic that the author created around himself among acquaintances and friends and that his alter egos create around themselves in his fictions.

A coda. While rereading Joyce to write this chapter, I found myself one morning—the occasion was a literary Festival in France—at lunch across the table from David Lodge. It seemed an opportunity too good to miss and I asked him his position on *Finnegans Wake*, explaining my own perplexity with the book. Lodge, who it turned out had taught *Finnegans Wake*, conceded that Joyce's novel required a huge effort on the part of the reader; he then added that thanks precisely to its notoriety any university seminar on the book was always well attended. In the light of this, Lodge concluded, it was hard not to feel that Joyce had found "a winning formula."

In just a few moments a conversation about Joyce had led to an assessment along the polarity winner/loser. Lodge did not say that he found *Finnegans Wake* a wonderful book or an engaging book or a profound book; his one observation was that Joyce had come up with a winning formula.

It is hard to think of a conversation about the other authors we shall look at in this book following that path.

Notes

1. James Joyce, *A Portrait of the Artist as a Young Man* (London: Jonathan Cape, 1924), chapter 2.
2. James Joyce, *Ulysses* (London: Penguin, 1968), 46. Hereafter cited as "*Ulysses*."
3. James Joyce, *Dubliners* (London: Jonathan Cape, 1967), 110. Hereafter cited as "*Dubliners*."
4. See, for example, Fritz Senn, "Righting Ulysses," in *James Joyce: New Perspectives* (Brighton: Harvester, 1982), 27.
5. Bernard Benstock (ed.), *Critical Essays on James Joyce* (Boston, MA: G. K. Hall, 1989), 9–27.

6. *A Tour of the Darkling Plain: The Finnegans Wake Letters of Thornton Wilder and Adaline Glasheen*, ed. Edward M. Burns and Joshua A. Gaylord (University College Dublin Press, 2001), p. xxi.

7. Samuel Beckett, "Dante … Bruno. Vico … Joyce," in *I can't go on, I'll go on* (New York: Grove Weidenfeld, 1976), 118.

8. *The Letters of Samuel Beckett, 1929–1940*, ed. M. D. Fehsenfeld, L. M. Overbeck, D. Gunn, and G. Craig (Cambridge University Press, 2009), 108.

9. Samuel Beckett, *Worstword Ho* (London: Calder, 1984), 22.

10. C. J. Jung, *The Spirit in Man, Art, and Literature*, Vol. 15 (New York: Pantheon, 1966), 113. Hereafter cited as "Jung."

4

Good Boy, Bad Boy

In these families...at the centre of the emotional dynamic is the conflict between good and evil.... conversation is organized around episodes which bring into play the intention to do harm, selfishness, greed, guilty pleasure, but also goodness, purity, innocence, asceticism, as well as sacrifice and abstinence. As a result, members of these families will feel, and be seen as, good, pure, responsible or alternatively bad, selfish, immoral. They will meet people who will save them, improve them, or, on the contrary, who will initiate them into vice, lead them to behaviour that will then make them feel guilty. They will marry people who are innocent, pure, capable of self-denial or, on the other hand, cruel egoists who will take advantage of them.... Some of them will suffer for their selfishness, and at times from the malice of others or for the intrinsic badness of their own impulses. Others will be proud of their own purity and moral superiority.

Valeria Ugazio, *Permitted and Forbidden Stories*, 128.

The publisher of this book has asked me to include a section on my own writing, to put myself in the picture. I do this with reluctance. My whole background, my personality, the position I usually assume, urges me not to.

Is this because, like Joyce, I believe the artist shouldn't descend into public debate, should remain detached, above, superior? Obviously not, otherwise I wouldn't have begun this book at all.

Is it because I am afraid of provoking ridicule by seeming to invite comparisons between myself and the distinguished names who are the objects of the other chapters? No. I am not afraid of criticism. I do my best not to read reviews and have learned not to worry about them. Nor am I afraid of comparisons. Let people think what they will. I'm not worried about the *risk* of self exposure, then, but I do feel it is *inappropriate*, it is putting myself forward too much, it is self regarding, it is *wrong*!

With that word we have it. I was brought up in a world where right and wrong were overwhelmingly the dominant criterion for judging everybody and everything, where right was altruism and self effacement and in poor supply while wrong was selfishness, affirmation, indulgence and more or less endemic. You can see, then, why Joyce's extravagant claims to grandeur even before he had published a word are bound to raise a frown from me. And indeed, if I placed the chapter on Joyce before this chapter, it was first to establish a method, before turning it on myself, and second because I could think of no greater foil to my approach to writing, and indeed the world in general, than Joyce's approach. After Joyce, my position can only come as a sharp contrast, and in describing my position and background my uneasiness with Joyce will become more explicable, and with it the idea that when writer and reader meet, we are not simply talking about questions of aesthetics. On the other hand, I wouldn't like anyone to suppose that my irony at the expense of Joyce's self importance means I don't have grandiose ambitions myself, that I don't think, or at least hope, that my own best can hold its own with the best of the best. It is simply that, in the normal way of things, I feel it is right to keep this to myself. I mustn't sing my praises. Hence my reluctance to begin this chapter. Hence, also, when it comes to the *way* I write, the style or styles I use, it would be unthinkable for me to draw attention to my ambitions as dramatically as Joyce does with the flagrantly look-at-me style of parts of *Ulysses* or *Finnegans Wake*. I have to work more stealthily, drawing less attention to myself as author. Again that doesn't mean the ambition isn't there. It doesn't mean that secretly I don't perhaps think I have written things rather *better* than *Finnegans Wake*.

Why do I insist on mentioning my ambition and including this, for some readers, preposterous claim? Because the semantic "right and wrong" demands that I *tell the truth about myself*, and that I must not lay claims to any virtue or modesty I don't have.

To summarize: I must not boast as Joyce did. But: I must openly admit, once goaded into talking about myself, that deep down I share the kind of megalomaniac ambition that made him boast. You can see this is a demanding system of values to work in. I would gladly be shot of it. It might be fun to write to other famous authors and tell them

I am more important than they are. Alas, I could never do that, not because virtuous or modest, but because that's how I am.

Let's start at the beginning.

My parents read to me as a child, so I understood at once that reading was something "good." Intensely evangelical, my father and mother—a clergyman and his wife—only did things that were good. They read us children's stories and they read the Bible. Later I exploited this faith of theirs in the goodness of literature to find relief there from the suffocating world of moral constriction in which they lived and wanted everyone else to live.

When they read to us, a daughter and two sons, perhaps by a crackling fire, with an evening cup of cocoa, the books created a feeling of togetherness; whether it was Pooh Bear or *The Secret Garden* or Biggles, we were united in one place in the thrall of one parental voice, my mother's usually, and afterwards there was a shared store of stories and memories that united us.

When I read alone, when I began to search out books that would broaden the narrow perspective they imposed, then books isolated me, and divided us. Now I had ideas and arguments that countered theirs. I read avidly, safe in the knowledge that they thought my being a reader was a good thing; I felt rather pleased with myself. But soon enough they picked up a copy of Gide, of Beckett, of Nietzsche, and then there were tears and conflict. Away from the Bible and children's books, reading was *not* always good. It was dangerous. I read even more avidly, but secretively now, careful that they shouldn't see what I was up to. I went underground, at least with the "bad" books. It was smart and chaste, on the other hand, to be seen to be reading Shakespeare or Swift. Which is odd, isn't it, when you think of all the things you can find in those authors? But they were national treasures. Goodness was patriotic. Or rather England was good. More virtuous still would have been to have a copy of C. S. Lewis always at hand. But I could never stomach C. S. Lewis. He was goody goody.

My father's study was wall to wall Bible concordances and theology and Christian testimony. I never opened one of them. The concordances in particular were huge tomes in scab red covers, suggesting dusty penitence. I tell a lie. I must have opened them once or twice because I remember their pages divided into two yellowing columns and peppered with text references, brackets, footnotes. A glance was enough to tell me I would never read them.

In the living room was a small rotating mahogany bookcase with an assortment of literature and children's books, anything from Dumas to Kingsley, Lewis Carroll to Sholokhov, *Three Men in a Boat* to John Buchan. They were permitted. I read them all.

Right at the back of the cubby hole under the stairs, where you had to get on your knees as the ceiling came down, wrapped in thick brown paper and tied in string, was a book published in the 1940s about marriage and sex; it included some instructions as to how to go about making love if you never had before. Things like: don't be in a hurry to get all your clothes off, and, think of your partner's pleasure as much as your own. This book, whose title I have forgotten, was hugely useful to me. It was also extremely interesting to discover that my righteous parents did this stuff. It was also interesting that the book could not appear on other shelves in the house. Also, it was fun learning how to undo the string and do it up again as if the package was still untouched since...since when? Presumably the time when my parents no longer felt they needed its wise advice. Anyway, the fact was, there were books that were good, or for the good, but not good for everyone at every moment. This was a development.

In my sister's room, painted pink with flowery curtains and a pink bedspread, the shelves were full of Georgette Heyer and similar dreamy romances of a historical flavour. At some point I must have noticed the relationship between the book covers and the room's decor. This was the aura my sister moved in. She played the guitar in church and was always prayerful and anything to do with romance came in a patina of propriety and pink. I once read about half of a Georgette Heyer novel. It was no help at all.

In the bookshelf in my brother's room, among sundry science fiction by Asimov and Ballard, not even hidden, was a paperback called *Lasso Round the Moon* by Agnar Mykle. Paperbacks were new to me. There was a photograph on the cover that left little to the imagination. I understood at once that only certain sections of this book need be read. They were already well thumbed.

It strikes me at once, remembering these early dealings with books, that they were inevitably divided in my mind, not so much in terms of well-written or badly written, exciting or boring, believable or unbelievable, but in relation to the dominant criterion for thinking of everything in our family, good or bad, innocent or dangerous. And as my mind shifted between nice books and nasty books and complicated combinations of the two, I put their styles and stories in relation to the members of the family. My father was good of course, but in an intellectual way, a bible concordance way, a way that wanted goodness and reason and study to be entirely compatible; a sermonizing way, if you like, for what did Father do with those concordances if not use them to write his sermons?

My mother was also good, if anything more intensely so than my father, but now goodness had to do with emotions, with sacrifice, with unselfishness, with expecting others not to let you down or hurt you by being bad. Mother cooked and cleaned and cared for you and you felt she did it with goodness in her heart. My father was angry if I was caught reading an evil book. My mother was hurt. I could deal with my father's anger any time. But not with my mother's pain. That was the problem.

My sister, if she found out, about *Lasso Round the Moon* for example, was indignant, scandalized. This wouldn't have worried me, on the contrary it was rather fun, were it not for the fact that she was inclined to tell tales. Hers was the indignation, it occurs to me now, of someone who would have liked to read something a little more exciting than Georgette Heyer but felt she mustn't. So if she told tales she did so out of envy. It is something she got over many years ago and would laugh at now.

My brother didn't care. My brother did what he wanted. Or rather, no. My brother *deliberately* read the books he shouldn't be reading. He did what they wanted him *not* to do. Not Gide and Nietzsche but Agnar Mykle and Anaïs Nin. My brother provoked. It was the provocation of someone who was happy to know he was considered to be on the evil side of the good/evil divide. Perhaps the truth was that having suffered from polio at an early age, having spent some months at death's door, my brother was not so worried as the rest of us about issues of propriety. What mattered to him was being alive. In any event and for whatever the reason, he was clearly at home with being a bad boy. It didn't worry him that his reading about Agnar Mykle's blond hero Ash feeling the breasts of big Norwegian women who always moaned and writhed under his powerful fingers made my mother writhe too, in a different way. She suffered. He didn't care. He didn't read dangerous things in secret, but *openly*. Perhaps he wouldn't have read them at all if there was no one to watch. He said the problem was mother's, not his. "Tell them to go fuck themselves," he would say when I was sent up to his room to remind him it was time for church. I was the messenger between the bad son and the good mother. That was my position, the intermediary. He was in bed reading a paperback. It had a dangerous cover: strewn clothes and naked bodies. "You can say I'm reading," he laughed. "They like reading." My brother's room was all dirty socks and T-shirts and guitars and amplifiers and the paintings he was making. The first contraceptive foil I ever saw was wedged between the canvas and the frame of one of my brother's paintings.

Transgression and art. There was definitely an affinity between Agnar Mykle's paperback covers and the way my brother kept his room, as there was between Georgette Heyer's frilly beauties and my sister's room. Only many years later did I look at Agnar Mykle again and realize he was actually quite a serious author, there were only a few pages of sex in the book. Maybe my brother wasn't just provoking after all. And only a couple of years ago, when an Italian publisher asked me to check a translation, did I reread a little Georgette Heyer and appreciate that she was something more than soft romance for a good girl who wanted a little badness. Maybe my sister wasn't so bereft. My childhood polarities had made the whole world black and white.

Except for myself, my grey self. It will seem all too easy, this fusion of topography and symbolism, but it's true: my room was sandwiched *between* my brother's and my sister's. It too had a bookshelf of course. There were no rosily-clad historical romances here. There were no girls clutching a last shred of modest clothing to their gorgeous cleavages. There were no concordances, no Christian testimonies. There were no innocent children's books. There were Tolstoy and Dostoevsky and Chekhov and Flaubert and Zola. These books were *foreign*, out of it. They had lots of interesting stuff in them, but my parents saw them as intellectual and hence possibly good, or at least not absolutely bad. They were a middle ground and an escape, into *seriousness*.

Three or four of the books on the top shelf of my bookcase were not there permanently; they came from the library. My parents loved us to go to the library; my father in particular had invested heavily in the intellect and, in line with Wycliffe and the Reform of five hundred years ago, encouraged any activity that had to do with respectable texts. My wonder was that in these quiet rooms off High Road, North Finchley novels were simply arranged in alphabetical order from the various Abbots to Zweig. The only way you could tell if a book was good or bad was by studying the cover and leafing about in it. Denying me my regular criterion, my simply *knowing* that if a book was to be found in a certain room of the house it would be of a certain kind, the library invited me into different areas of meaning, choice, and responsibility. I felt lost and happy there.

Meantime it had become clear to me that, when the time came, I would study literature, I would move into this other world of words that had meaning to me not only in itself but for the special position it was giving me in the family, the position of someone reading books that could not easily be described as good or bad, of someone who wanted to say, not that good or bad didn't exist, but that the world was *more complicated* than that. And because this was *true*, or I felt it was, how could it not be a good thing to say it? I wasn't being bad. I was shifting goodness away from innocence and self sacrifice towards *truth*. Because it suited me.

Even before studying literature formally, at school and university, I had already gained some experience in text analysis. Every Wednesday evening there was a Young People's Bible study in the curate's house. We read a short passage from the Bible with the curate and discussed it at length. Was I forced to go to these meetings? Not exactly. But it would have looked bad if I didn't go. It would have been discouraging for everyone if the vicar's son didn't go to Bible study. Or rather if *neither of the vicar's sons* went. My mother would have looked disappointed and forlorn, my father displeased and vexed. "You are allowing yourself to be influenced by your brother," they would say. "You are aping your brother." In a way I couldn't not go to Bible study precisely because my brother already didn't go and I wasn't going to be the one to strike my mother this second blow. Perhaps if he had gone I wouldn't have had to.

But I looked on the bright side. There were girls at the Bible study. There were ankles and blouses and smiles. By concentrating on the words, you could show them you were clever. Girls drove me crazy.

You could show them you had an interesting position, neither fervent nor hostile. Verse after verse we dissected the Scriptures. What did it mean "In the beginning was the Word?" What did it mean that "the Holy Spirit proceedeth from the Father and the Son," that "the meek shall inherit the earth," that "no man cometh to the Father but by me"? I still remember the day we tackled the passage, "I know thy works, that thou art neither cold nor hot: I would thou wert cold or hot. So then because thou art lukewarm, and neither cold nor hot, I will spue thee out of my mouth." At once I experienced a shiver of recognition: that was me. The middle position wasn't better than the good position, as I hoped. It was worse than the bad position. Lukewarm was worse than cold. I experienced a crisis. For a while I tried to be more enthusiastically on the good side, not to leaf through *Lasso Round the Moon*, not to fantasize the ankles and the blouses, but this was hard because it was as if I was not really living. I was denying myself the only things that seemed to give life real energy. Sometimes I would be in a complete frenzy about this. I absolutely needed to do something bad. Masturbate, smoke, get drunk, feel a girl's legs. I would play hours of football so as not to think about it. Years later, reading Ugazio's book on semantic polarities, I recognized that I had always been in the median position, always found it difficult to understand where I stood on all this. What made it more irritating was that everyone else in the family was so sure of themselves; they all knew *exactly* where they stood in relation to each other. I envied my brother his easy transgressions, my sister her confident virtue. The only compensation for my uncertainty, on occasion, was a sweet taste of superiority. I understood *the problem*, and they didn't.

Naturally it was always a pleasure to be away from home, daily at school, then for long periods at the university. Naturally my favourite lesson was English, literature. I was excited and grateful for the tools of analysis teachers put in our hands. It was helpful to understand a little better how the words were working together. But I sensed at once that something was wrong. Why were we never to talk about the authors themselves and the role the books played in their lives? There was always a red line through your essay if you presumed to reflect on the genesis of the story. And why did we never talk about readers, about which people read which books and why some books were clearly written for a certain kind of person—my sister, my brother—

and other books seemingly for nobody, unless perhaps the author himself. Above all, why could you never speak about your personal reaction, why you disliked a book maybe, even a classic; why you had good reasons for disliking it, or thought you did, and why even when you didn't have good reasons for disliking it, nevertheless, uncannily, you went on disliking it, intensely, despite the fact that all the authorities had deemed this text sublime. Try to put that in your school exercise book and there was another red line. Oddly, the *study* of literature systematically excluded the *experience* of literature.

I did pretty well in my school English classes, but in 1970, aged 16, I received a fail mark for my essay on *The Love Song of J. Alfred Prufrock*. "Biographical fallacy!" the teacher declared at the bottom of the page. I had written that T. S. Eliot's sophisticated rendering of one man's depressing inadequacy with women suggested an author trying to compensate for his own failings by turning them into a clever literary performance. For this, as I supposed, astuteness I had expected an A and instead got a D. From a teacher who liked me! "Never mix up an author's work with his life," he growled. Many years later I read Peter Ackroyd's biography of Eliot and discovered that I had been right. How could it have been otherwise?

But my teacher was also right. At university nothing was considered more wrong-headed, more crass and naïve than putting an author's work in relation to his life. One was to analyse structures, stylemes, patterns of imagery and symbolism, but never to reflect that the author might be writing about matters of urgent concern to himself. Even more confusing, studying at Cambridge under David Holbrook, disciple of F. R. Leavis, I had fallen into the hands of someone who insisted on taking a strong moral position on works of literature, insisting that they *be* moral, putting that criterion at the top and making morality indivisible from aesthetics; naturally this immediately made sense to me with where I was coming from; it was even encouraging in a way, since Holbrook's morality was not my parents' morality, was not attached to any metaphysics, or submission to the pathos of a Christ who had died for my sins, etc. It was a difficult, intelligent morality. However, even in this case one was still not supposed to relate the work to the author's life or to your own in any way, which now seemed even more bizarre, since a sense of moral urgency can only come out of a situation, an experience, a *life*.

While at university I began my first experiments with writing of my own. Perhaps inevitably I took as my guide the various literary techniques we had been learning to analyse in great works of literature. I remembered that in serious novels there were always many layers of meaning; this phenomenon was a guarantee of quality and I tried to work it in. I tried to lay down patterns of symbolism, and hidden lexical fields in some special relation to that symbolism. Finally I would seek to integrate all this with the sort of plot that works out in an unexpected way, or doesn't quite work out, leaving the reader hanging, etc. All very deliberately.

In short, I was in danger of becoming one of those writers who *knows how to write*, knows how to create literature, meaning literature as the literary critical establishment understands it, literature made to be analysed by people who know how to analyse literature, and so on. You put something together thinking of someone else who will take it apart. It's a form destined to become cerebral, locked into itself, detached, as each writer learns to do what literature has done before, regardless of the experience he is living, a phenomenon driven only by ambition, bereft of life. A large percentage of what passes for literature today is of this kind, perhaps with brief moments of genuine perception, genuine freshness. In the end the academic study of literature, becoming prescriptive as it inevitably did, but also absurdly celebrative—as if literature were the most important thing in the world—was bound to kill literature, to turn it into a ghost of itself, always repeating the same gestures in the same costumes, a place the reader goes for escape, or to exercise his puzzle-cracker's ability of analysing literature. In general, we are all too eager, even anxious to write, and to feel that what we have written is *literature*.

Fortunately, I was no good at it. Submitting a story as an optional addition to my Part One exams I was awarded a Third. Overall I had a First. I was a good critic but no good at the creative side. Perhaps I should accept that. Yet more and more only the creative side interested me. This too had to do with my background. For if one rejects the fierce Manichaeanism of my parents' thinking, yet at the same time keeps enough of one's conditioning to need to think of oneself as good, one has to do it, reject the Manichaeanism I mean, not in the name of transgression, but of seriousness, of a deep involvement in life. And if literature becomes something detached and cerebral, it won't do. Literature was only possible for me, from where I was coming, if one poured life into it, poured in the struggle to find a position in a swirl of emotions and ideas that were always inseparable from certain experiences and certain people.

Much of this was obscure to me at the time, but one thing was absolutely clear and remains so: when it came to that awful moment when a young man has to decide what to do to make money and live an independent life, I found to my surprise that the *only* thing I could really envisage myself doing, or doing *happily*, I mean with a feeling of self realization, was writing. And this I knew at once had to do with my father and with all the sermons I had listened to throughout my youth, the sermons spun from those concordances. I would not follow in his footsteps exactly. But nor would I exactly oppose him. I would write books that *undid* his sermons and certainties, books that returned life to the great confusion I always felt it was before he preached about it. In a classically unhelpful move, I would draw people into my own state of anxiety and excitement over these matters.

Finishing my degree at Cambridge and shifting to Harvard not so much to study as to escape home, I began to look for a way to write that didn't involve constructing literature from the theories I'd learned, but was not simply in opposition to them either. All attention must go to what the *real* sensations and conundrums of life are. But how difficult that is! How difficult it is to observe sensations honestly, to write about them effectively, and how difficult to merge this with some practical project of getting published and making money in a world where people have certain expectations of books enshrined in conventions which are attractive in their way. But somehow or other money would have to be made, since my family had none.

It was an endless process of hit and miss, or rather miss and miss, that lasted eight years. Years in which I first returned to London, worked in offices and language schools, married an Italian girl I had met at Harvard, and moved to Italy in 1981. All the time I was trying to write, trying not to accept an "ordinary" career. Perhaps from my background I had also learned the ludicrous idea of being somehow *chosen*. I knew that this could not rationally be the case. All the same I kept on trying when it might have seemed more sensible to stop. It is quite possible not to believe something intellectually but to act as if one did emotionally. And emotions always trump the intellect when it comes to action.

With each new novel, in those early days, I worked by imitating some style I was taken with, then seeking to feel the tension between that style and my own perceptions and adjust accordingly; as a result my writing became as it were a position developed in relation to a position I had felt some affinity for. Henry Green, Samuel Beckett, Elizabeth Bowen, Beryl Bainbridge, were all writers who seemed to offer things I needed, though the first two were too powerful an influence—one could only succumb and copy, badly—while the second two left too much space for me to lose myself. It was hard going. I wrote seven novels and a score of stories without publication.

Not surprisingly the book that broke through, after interminable rejections, was a little autobiographical novel about an adolescent caught between opposites in an evangelical family that becomes involved in the charismatic movement: for that is an episode of my family life I haven't mentioned, the story of how my parents, who had once read Pooh Bear to us, now cast out demons and spoke in tongues. Needless to say, this development had pushed the tensions in the family to the limit. It was a short book written in a style I had learned from the Italian writer Natalia Ginzburg, a laconic, detached, adolescent first person spoken by one who feels they shouldn't really have been part of the events described, or who would have been glad to have been spared them, one who looks back on childhood with a sense of unhappy wonder. Perhaps the advantage of being influenced by narrative written and read in a foreign language is that one learns a mood and a manner, but is not in danger of aping the exact words or syntax. The plot of my novel culminated in a true event, the climax of the opposition between my brother and my parents when they and my sister tried to exorcize him in our front room. It was a drama from which I was carefully excluded, up in my bedroom, reading Chekhov perhaps. In the novel I invented some involvement on my part that saved the day for my brother. It was wishful thinking.

"I could never write a book like that," a friend of mine, himself a novelist, told me on reading *Tongues of Flame*. "I would be too afraid of my mother's reaction." Here we are then with the issue of a novel's effect on immediate friends and family and the way predicting that effect may tense and guide, or in any event condition the act of writing.

However, the truth, at least in this case, was that I had received so many rejections by the time I wrote *Tongues of Flame*—literally hundreds—that I worked on the book almost without restraint, writing it over just a couple of months. I had ceased to believe I would be published. I was free. Collecting a score of rejections over two or three years in which I wrote other things, this novel eventually came runner-up in a prize for unpublished manuscripts; the jury recommended the book to the publisher sponsoring the prize, they agreed to publish (despite having previously rejected the book) and sent the typescript to my agent, who had herself also rejected the book but had been in contact with the same publisher about other attempts of mine. This agent, not wanting to spend on phone-calls or postage to Italy, promptly sent the typescript to my mother's London address, with a letter explaining that it would be published. Under instructions to open any business mail, my mother read the letter, was delighted for me, read the book and was terribly upset.

There we are. I had finally hurt my mother in a big way, far worse a way, come to think of it, than anything my brother had ever managed. And done it with my pen. There were long and expensive phone conversations full of tears on her part. Overall, though, I realized that hurting others wasn't as hard as I had thought it would be, especially if you were getting your book published. She wanted me to withdraw it. I offered to publish under a pseudonym to save her the embarrassment (my father had died some years before). However, on advice from friends and publisher, I changed my mind and published under my own name. This was *my* life, *my* career, I had waited a long time. There was nothing, I thought, untrue or seriously offensive in the book. And in fact, in the end, my mother put it behind her. Or was willing to say she had. It was part of her vocation for sacrifice. From this point on, however, there would be a tense awareness that what I wrote would impact on those around me, that I would find it hard to feel I was "a good person" if I hurt others by the things I published. At the same time it did seem to me that novels were the kind of space where one needed to be free to explore the most difficult things, the most intimate experiences. This was and remains a conundrum.

I will not talk about my novels that deal with marriage. *Goodness, Europa, Destiny, Judge Savage, Cleaver.* "Parks's nearest and dearest," wrote the novelist Patrick Gale, reviewing one of these (*Goodness*, I think) "must await each of his publications with growing trepidation." For Gale, part of the experience of reading my novels had become a wondering about their genesis and consequences. The story on the page hints at a life story beyond. Here one might mention Bateson again; thinking about ritual and art, their functions in society, he had suggested that any long-term intimate relationship, or indeed any really stable social relationship, depended on the mutual respect of both partners for a taboo, or many taboos; it was precisely the agreed silence about core facts that allowed a relationship to become, as it were, chronic, or, looking at it more positively, stable. In this vision, rituals and art offered the relief of allowing the taboo to surface, acknowledged, but in coded form. So, for the poet or novelist, always assuming Bateson is on to something here, writing offers a way of smuggling a message through a taboo, while leaving the taboo intact, threatening to break it—"this is the truth about our marriage"—but not *quite* breaking it—"actually this is only a novel and I don't really think this is the truth about our marriage at all."

But for the purposes of illustrating the relation of my work to the ideas I am developing here, I want to say a few words about a different kind of novel, one that some might say was written with the left hand, though I'm not sure that the kind of hierarchy that metaphor implies is appropriate; that is, I would agree that the novel was written with my left hand if we accept that the left hand is not merely an inferior right hand, but rather a *different* hand that has functions all its own, functions the right hand could not carry out. The left hand is as much *me* as the right.

In my eagerness to publish, between ages 24 and 30, I had experimented in genre writing. A novel call *Leo's Fire* about an arson ring in Boston (where I had studied) was shortlisted for the BBC Arrow Prize. Publication was not offered when it was learned that I was not, as was the first-person narrator, a crippled black American. A thriller about Italian terrorists, *The Palace of Justice*, was accepted by an agent and received generous rejection slips. The last of these left-handed attempts was *Cara Massimina*, which nodded to Patricia Highsmith's Ripley books, but tried, consciously, to bring to the psycho-crime mix two novelties: my deeper knowledge of Italy and comedy. What I really brought to the story, unconsciously, was my background; I had grown up in a world where, of course, crime fits, is attractive even—it is sin, self indulgence, excitement—but where nevertheless one would do anything not to think of oneself as a criminal. So the special achievement of my hero, Morris Duckworth, would be to become a multiple murderer while remaining convinced that he was essentially a good person and that his victims deserved their deaths and anyway, from the afterlife, forgave him his crimes.

None of this was planned. It came out page by page, improvising in exactly the same way my hero improvised, never planning his crimes but flying entirely by the seat of his pants, or rather the author's pants as I sat at a desk with a small manual typewriter. Freed of the "seriousness" of my other novels (*Tongues of Flame* and various others were already gathering rejections) I was having fun. Writing straight onto the typewriter was part of this. The more "serious" novels required silence and a sharp pencil. In a sense, then, the book itself was a crime against my serious vocation, an indulgence that would probably never be read (I was still unpublished) as the hero's murders were never to be discovered. And since it was the first book I had attempted directly on a typewriter it was, in a very practical way, written with the left hand *as well as* the right.

But to the plot.

Much attached to his pious mother who died in his teens, Morris Duckworth, a virgin, flees England and above all his heavy-drinking, lascivious, working-class father to become an English teacher in Verona. Previously, he had been expelled from Cambridge when caught in possession of some marijuana that another person had asked him to look after at a party. Innocent but found guilty, he is understandably aggrieved, convinced that had he had contacts in high places, or simply come from a better school, he would not have been expelled. In Italy, teaching English in private evening classes, he feels he is underachieving, he deserves better. Nobody notices his genius. But he has learned to speak Italian.

> [T]he only thing he had truly gained these last two years was the ability to speak a foreign language near perfectly and the curious freedom that ability now appeared to give him in the way he thought. As if he had shifted off rails. His mind seemed to roam free now over any and every possibility. He must make a big

effort always to think in Italian as well as speak it, Morris thought. It could be a way out of himself and out of the trap they had all and always wanted him to fall into.[1]

These few lines, written again without any consciousness of what I was up to, perhaps say a great deal about my own decision to remain in Italy. Although this country, when you get to know it, is the least free of places, nevertheless, the movement to another language releases you from a number of inhibitions that you now appreciate are actually coded into your native tongue, or better still your mother tongue, the English my mother taught me to speak.

What Morris likes about the Bel Paese is its traditions and its old art. Its heavy decorum, its discreet and elegant wealth. And you feel at once, though I was unaware of this as I wrote it, that Morris is replacing his mother's exacting vision of selfless goodness with a more comfortable notion of aesthetics and respectability. Art is good and allows for luxury too, especially as it manifests itself in Italian style; in this sense Morris is in tune with the great Renaissance bankers who made the austere medieval church comfortable for themselves by filling it with art. On a train, thinking and speaking in Italian, Morris commits his first crime, stealing an object of Italian style, a Gucci document case. Its owner is in the bathroom when the train stops in a provincial station. Morris gets off the train with the case. Finding inside a diary that gives different girls' names on different days he suspects its owner, who had said he was married, of having various mistresses, or seeing prostitutes. This entirely justifies Morris's decision to steal the document case, and even to write a couple of threatening letters to the owner in an attempt to extort money. The attempt fails miserably.

A 17-year-old schoolgirl taking lessons from Morris falls in love with his handsome blondness and evidently troubled character. Morris courts her, Massimina, less out of lust or love—his sexuality, with pious mother on one side and lecherous father on the other is completely repressed—but because she offers a road, not just to wealth, but to that very special, staid and stylish wealth of the Italian provinces. What Morris seems to be seeking (all this in retrospect) is a luxury that is also penitential, that satisfies his needs to be good and bad simultaneously. Here he is arriving in his *fidanzata*'s out of town palazzo.

In many respects the sitting room was very much like the dining room—heavily furnished and dark with an overwhelming sense of straight lines and woodenness about it. This was certainly not the nouveau riche. The floor was marble, black-and-white chequerboard squares, the furniture painfully upright in coffin-quality mahogany, while ivies of the more sombre kind trailed dark leaves across a tiger rug (genuine down to the bullet hole). Yet surprisingly, the old-fashioned curiosity of the room put Morris at his ease, rather than the opposite. It was the theatricality of the place. How could you feel responsible for anything said in a room like this? And especially if it was said in Italian. He sat down on a viciously straight-backed chair, careful not to jerk his head too much lest dandruff should sift down onto his jacket. (*Massimina*, chapter 3)

Precisely Morris's new-found freedom, speaking in Italian, leads him to talk up his career prospects a little with a few white lies to his *fidan-zata*'s mother and two older sisters. Alas, Massimina's conservative family check up on him. He is found out and banished. Massimina is withdrawn from her classes. Morris gnashes his teeth in outer darkness. He has tried to move from England to Italy, from one ethos to another, to find a place where he can feel good but also complacent, and he has failed.

But Massimina is in love and will not give up on her man. Running away from home, she comes to Morris just as lessons end and summer begins. She has brought all her savings, she hasn't told her parents where she is going. The author and Morris have the book's central idea at the same moment: take her away on holiday and write a ransom letter back to her family *as if she had been kidnapped*. So Morris sets out on a journey that will require all his ingenuity, not only to keep the girl hidden while not understanding that she is being hidden, not only to prevent her from being in touch with her family without her appreciating she is being thus prevented, but also to find ways to convince himself that what he is doing is not evil. Inevitably, the justification he falls back on is the notion of his intellectual, even aesthetic, superiority.

Ingenuity was the thing. That was what it was all about and that was what would make it forgivable in the end. The sheer brilliance. It wouldn't hurt them to part with a little of this world's goods. Even the inspector had said that, more or less. It might damn well do them some good in fact. And if it gave the signora some twinges of remorse over how she had brought up and handled her children (not to mention how she had handled Morris), then all well and good.

He would give a tenth of the money to charity anyway. That should look good if it ever came to selling his story to the Mirror. Kidnapper tithes booty. No, the fact was he was a generous person, if only he had had something to be generous with...
(*Massimina*, chapter 9)

Morris hides the girl on the beach at Rimini. Who would look among the sunshades and the crowds for a kidnap victim? But Massimina likes meeting people and befriends a Veronese photographer and his English girlfriend. The photographer, older than the others, with an evil grin and a bad leg (like my brother!), suggests partner swapping. Morris is appalled. There is also the fact that he has begun to enjoy Massimina's company, they have begun to touch each other and find a little physical pleasure together. Love seems on the cards. Now this horrible man is suggesting group sex. When the same man also realizes that Massimina is being reported as kidnapped and attempts to intervene, his fate is sealed. With only seconds to cast about for a murder weapon, Morris can reassure himself that he is doing no more than crushing a cockroach. The euphoria of getting away with it leads to first sex with Massimina...

I was 28. I had meant to write a genre novel, as a sort of exercise, or amusement, as part of a desire to publish. Starting the book I had no idea of the plot, no idea if I would bother finishing it. Yet looking back it's clear that I created a hero who was extremely personal, one who would establish a very particular relationship with the reader, a relationship that would then re-emerge in more "serious" novels like *Goodness* and *Cleaver*. Morris is a loathsome person, he really is. But it's evident that the author sympathizes with him, to a degree, gives energy and charm to him, never openly criticizes him. So the reader begins to feel divided; he identifies with Morris and the slapstick excitement of his harmless early crimes, but then is shocked when things start to get serious. Yet Morris remains seductive. It's hard to want him to be caught. And the novel pushes this emotional conundrum to the limit, at once making Morris evil, worse than evil in his insistent presentation of himself as good, yet entertaining, always more attractive, witty, and intelligent than his victims, and so on. As if wittiness could stand in for better behaviour. The novel, that is, without any conscious plan on my part to do this, begins to draw the reader into a state of mind where good and evil are absolutely the dominant criteria, but we are confused as to where we stand, we desire some reconciliation between the two poles, a reconciliation that, once Morris has killed, will be impossible. This desire for reconciliation is also evident in the comedy of the story; the farce is so grotesque that the good/evil polarity seems absurd, unnecessary; it surely can't be necessary to kidnap and kill in order to enjoy life, in order to begin to have a physical relationship with a woman. The forced nature of the whole story suggests a desire that this not be true.

Cara Massimina was accepted by my agent but widely rejected by publishers. Once the very different *Tongues of Flame* was published, and then other "serious" novels, I put it aside. But years later, chatting to a novelist who writes crime thrillers (the same who told me that he couldn't write something like *Tongues of Flame* for fear of what his mother would say), I mentioned that I had once had a go at crime writing myself. He insisted I dig out the manuscript, read it, was enthusiastic, and encouraged me to publish. I feared that the difference in tone and style and apparent ambition between this book and the four others I had now published would perhaps undermine the reputation I hoped I was building up. Hence I offered the novel under the pseudonym of John MacDowell. Again it's with some amazement that I realize (only *now*, setting that name down in this context) that it contains the family polarity in a nutshell. For John was my brother, on the "bad" side and MacDowell my mother's maiden name on the "good." Even a maiden name has a certain place in this force field. Having renounced a pseudonym then for *Tongues of Flame*, a work that I felt was serious, but that hurt my mother, I was now using one for a work that slightly embarrassed me as being possibly an evasion from seriousness, a sort of silly self indulgence. I was wrong to do this, wrong in the sense of mistaken; because the work was very much to do with me, and again because it was rather successful, and finally because, precisely in its wishing to make a farce of the polarity I had emerged from, it was also deadly serious.

Cara Massimina was published in a dozen countries and well received, particularly in the States, where the *Los Angeles Times* found it "better than *Silence of the Lambs*." In this period, when I was still reading reviews, what struck me was the difference between those who simply enjoyed the plot, the humour, and those who clearly felt threatened and shocked by Morris Duckworth, or rather by the way he was presented, as if his dilemma between good and evil, between killing and not killing, were something we could joke about. These readers—and their reviews were extremely aggressive and unpleasant—wanted to insist that the moral aspect of the novel be taken more seriously. I have no doubt that these were people coming from the same semantic I came from, people for whom it simply was not right to present good and evil at once so intensely and so lightly. I understood them perfectly and felt rather guilty, though I did think that they might also have realized that one aim of the book was precisely to savour the scandal of taking morality lightly, precisely to have everybody agree that we shouldn't do this. In two cases the same reviewers had responded very positively to *Tongues of Flame*.

Film rights to the book were bought by Dennis Potter, who produced a script and alas died before he could make it into a film. Fascinating about his script was that he too refused to take the combination of killing and farce to the limit, sparing Massimina at the end of the book, as if it had been a mistake on my part to push slapstick into nightmare. These were the days before *Pulp Fiction*. What I am suggesting is that, aside from any question of the quality of the writing, there are elements in the background of the readers that condition their reaction, making the story acceptable or unacceptable as the case may be. Potter, who found my denouement unacceptable, was nevertheless fascinated by the novel's tensions. Any consideration of his plays suggests that his mind moved in the same force field as mine. It is precisely the person for whom the book "makes sense" who will be shocked by it. For others it was simply a dark farce.

But let's return a moment to *Cara Massimina* and my relationship with Italy. We have seen how Joyce lived in three European countries without ever engaging deeply in their daily life, remaining forever turned homeward towards Dublin where all his work is set. In a consideration of Lawrence in a later chapter we will see how the foreign countries he lived in were to provide him with an exciting "otherness" that would stimulate both trepidation and courage, offering him experiences of a more natural, even primitive, way of living than he could find in an over-sophisticated England. Unlike Joyce, he wrote about these countries, but as a traveller; he never really dug down into them, never stayed long enough to go native. My desire on the other hand, like Morris's in *Cara Massimina*, has always been to immerse myself in Italy and things Italian. Not initially because I "loved" Italian culture, but because it offered a space free of the protestant atmosphere I had grown up in; then more simply because this was the life around me. I could not imagine a scenario where I lived in a place but was not deeply involved in it. I have to be involved. Not necessarily to *belong*, I don't try to pass myself off as Italian, but to be engaged in what is going on. One of the problems of the kind of mental world my parents propagated is that intense living, loving, enjoying, is almost always seen to be on the evil side of the polarity; it is hard to get deep into life and be good; rather life itself becomes, as it is for Morris, a crime. I have done my best here in Italy, to become part of the fizz and bustle of everything around me. And like Morris I frequently have nightmares of being caught out and punished. As if just my living here were a sin.

Five years after publishing *Cara Massimina*, again in a break between two very taxing, rather experimental novels, *Shear* and *Europa*, I wrote a sequel to *Cara Massimina*, *Mimi's Ghost*. This was more obviously a farce than the first, with Morris now married to Massimina's older sister, but in communication with the dead Massimina's ghost, who now guides him, he supposes, in his crimes and whose spitting image he finds in Fra Lippo Lippi's *Madonna with Child* in the Uffizi. Again events precipitate; Morris constantly has to cover up his past, what he really is. Again the woman Morris is with is one of the victims. Again reviews divided exactly as for the first book. Again I felt vaguely guilty for having written something so frivolous, something described by all those who liked it with collocations like "deliciously amoral."

Only three years ago, so more than a decade after *Mimi's Ghost*, the critic Christopher Ricks told me he saw no difference in seriousness between these novels and the others. He pointed out that there was still a third sister for Morris to marry and/or murder and asked me if there would ever be the last of what seemed to him must be a trilogy.

I had in fact often thought of this, but it seemed too much of an indulgence to waste more time on Morris Duckworth. Now however a very *serious* man whom I much respected was suggesting this wasn't mere indulgence. This was me. Or rather it was indulgence and for me indulgence is a serious matter. So I began the last part of the trilogy, *Painting Death*.

This time, rereading the previous two books before beginning the third, I felt I finally understood what they were about. So as well as being another murder story cum farce, *Painting Death* also offers some reflection on the way art can serve, in a certain mind set, both to sublimate and justify certain impulses. Hardly a new idea. Morris, long married to the last of the three sisters, and now a successful businessman with two children, has for years been collecting paintings showing murders, often getting copies made of famous masterpieces. He hangs them in what was intended to be the ballroom of his wife's palazzo home. Here he is admiring a newly acquired copy of Delacroix's *Sardanapalus*:

> In winter, Morris liked to illuminate the grand room with real candelabra: four wonderfully baroque, wrought-iron monstrosities holding eighteen candles each. It took almost fifteen minutes to light them, lifting and lowering each circle of flame with a system of chains and pulleys, but the work was well worth it: the room became so much more exciting in their wayward, smoky flickering, with raised knives, hammers and broad swords quivering all around. Standing in front of *Sardanapalus*, with its bearded sadists and naked concubines, Morris enjoyed the strangely gratifying impression of being simultaneously in church and brothel.[2]

Morris is aware of the possible function of these paintings in his life:

> Perhaps I collect these paintings so as not to kill again; that thought flashed through his mind. Or perhaps because I'd love to kill again but don't have the nerve.
>
> A cannibal who wants to have his corpse and eat it. (p. 58)

Still frustrated, however, still convinced he is undervalued, Morris has the idea of sponsoring a major art exhibition focusing on paintings of brutal killing. This megalomania is justified as being essentially didactic in nature: if Morris has something to give to the world, it is his knowledge of what murder is about. At one point, and here again the unconscious had clicked in, this sense of what Morris knows and what paintings tell us about killing is linked to marriage. Our hero is in bed with his wife of twenty years; the couple now live in a state of mutual, sexless incomprehension:

> Suddenly, lying in this poignant silence between himself and his wife, it struck Morris with extraordinary force that murder was the moment when the dam broke and the truth about your nearest and dearest burst forth. Two people—Cain and Abel, Agamemnon and Clytemnestra, Othello and Desdemona— who had lived together in growing tension and distance, were finally revealed to one another. The horror on the victim's face was not just the horror of one about to die, that was nothing, but of someone who finally understands what has lain hidden for so long in his beloved's psyche. Yes! Or there was Romney's Medea where she is looking at her children and you can *see* what she's thinking. They are playing innocently, naked of course, and she is full of fury, full of murder. And the dam is cracking. The inhibitions are going. If I can't kill my husband I'll kill *them*! Good! Any moment now she's going to jump up and strike.
>
> This was what his art show would really be about, Morris realised: the moment of truth between two people, of awful truth, the rending of the veil that hides our unforgivable selves from each other. And Morris would be making that statement, talking about that issue, which was supremely *his* issue, but without actually quite giving away his own personal truth.
>
> How brilliant! God!
>
> All at once Morris Duckworth felt so pleased with himself he squeezed his wife's hand tight.
>
> "Oh Morris!" she murmured.
>
> "*Carissima*," he sighed. Full of affection he pushed his face blindly through the dark and kissed her hair.
>
> "How sweet," she whispered. "What on earth was that for?"
> (p. 78)

Enough. Readers will understand what I am getting at. The polarity which saturated the atmosphere in which I grew up is still present, both in the decision to write the book, in the content of the book, and in the relationship the book sets up with the reader. This is not, please, a statement on the quality of the writing, for which I make no claims.

Notes

1. Tim Parks, *Cara Massimina* (London: Vintage, 2011) 11. Hereafter cited as "*Massimina.*"
2. Tim Parks, *Painting Death* (London: Harvill Secker, 2014), 45.

5

The Reader's Address

I have spoken about the way background and in particular the values that dominated one's formative years influence every aspect of the process of storytelling, to the point that in my case one might see the kind of stories I tell in terms of the force field of meanings generated between the poles good and evil. We're not talking, for heaven's sake, about a *battle* between good and evil, something that could occur in more or less any story. Rather it's a question of the story itself coming out of the protagonist's and perhaps author's *uncertainty as to where he stands in that force field*, whether the one pole really is good and the other pole really is evil, an uncertainty, in turn, that has to do with the relationships formed in early life. Having talked, then, about my writing, I would like to say a word about how such a background influences the way one reads, the way one reacts to different writers.

It is now a commonplace to say that every reader reads a different book, yet little is said of particular readers and particular readings. Rather critics continue to produce readings that they hope will be authoritative, without saying anything about their own subjectivity and how it is structured. It's as if a line had been drawn beyond which a personal opinion is merely a mystery, a caprice, something we could not account for. All too frequently critics offer essay collections in which all the authors under consideration are already safely in the canon or at least widely celebrated, treating all of them with the same enthusiasm or indifference as if the question of "liking" one more than another were neither here nor there. So no risk is taken, no personal preference is exposed to discussion, while the reassuring impression is given that *we are all agreed* as to which writers are good and which are not. Inevitably, such essays have little life, since there is no struggle towards the truth of the essayist's personal reaction.

Just occasionally, however, someone does say clearly that this is not how things are, that I, the reader, stand in a special relation to what is on the page, and that this relation has to be discussed. Here, for example, is the full text of H. G. Wells's letter to Joyce, a few lines of which were quoted in a previous chapter. The two had recently met for the first time and the opening of Wells's response suggests that Joyce, as was his fashion, had asked a favour of the Englishman to whom he had given the opening chapters of *Finnegans Wake*.

My dear Joyce:

I've been studying you and thinking over you a lot. The outcome is that I don't think I can do anything for the propaganda of your work. I have enormous respect for your genius dating from your earliest books and I feel now a great personal liking for you but you and I are set upon absolutely different courses. Your training has been Catholic, Irish, insurrectionary; mine, such as it was, was scientific, constructive and, I suppose, English. The frame of my mind is a world wherein a big unifying and concentrating process is possible (increase of power and range by economy and concentration of effort), a progress not inevitable but interesting and possible. That game attracted and holds me. For it, I want a language and statement as simple and clear as possible. You began Catholic, that is to say you began with a system of values in stark opposition to reality. Your mental existence is obsessed by a monstrous system of contradictions. You may believe in chastity, purity and the personal God and that is why you are always breaking out into cries of cunt, shit and hell. As I don't believe in these things except as quite personal values my mind has never been shocked to outcries by the existence of water closets and menstrual bandages—and undeserved misfortunes. And while you were brought up under the delusion of political suppression I was brought up under the delusion of political responsibility. It seems a fine thing for you to defy and break up. To me not in the least.

Now with regard to this literary experiment of yours. It's a considerable thing because you are a very considerable man and you have in your crowded composition a mighty genius for expression which has escaped discipline. But I don't think it gets anywhere. You have turned your back on common men—on their elementary needs and their restricted time and intelligence, and you have elaborated. What is the result? Vast riddles. Your last two works have been more amusing and exciting to write than they will ever be to read. Take me as a typical common reader. Do I get much pleasure from this work? No. Do I feel I am getting something new and illuminating as I do when I read Anrep's dreadful translation of Pavlov's badly written book on Conditioned Reflexes? No. So I ask: Who the hell is this Joyce who demands so many waking hours of the few thousand I have still to live for a proper appreciation of his quirks and fancies and flashes of rendering?

All this from my point of view. Perhaps you are right and I am all wrong. Your work is an extraordinary experiment and I would go out of my way to save it from destructive or restrictive interruption. It has its believers and its following. Let them rejoice in it. To me it is a dead end.

My warmest wishes to you Joyce. I can't follow your banner any more than you can follow mine. But the world is wide and there is room for both of us to be wrong.

Yours,

H. G. Wells

(Ellmann, 607)

Wells connects background to style and content in his own work and to his reaction to other styles, other contents, other backgrounds. He separates writerly achievement from reader-gratification. He does not want to undermine the enthusiasm of Joyce's supporters but cannot join them. He sees both backgrounds as "illusion" and accepts that his "illusion" makes it hard for him to appreciate work coming out of a different "illusion," or indeed to find the time and patience for it.

It might seem, then, that in encountering Joyce's work, H. G. Wells comes up against what we previously described as an enigmatic episode, one that is not sufficiently interesting for him to want to overcome or open himself to; much easier just to put Joyce aside. Yet though Wells is correct in seeing how and why the polarities purity/ impurity, authority/insurrection are visible in Joyce's writing, he is

surely wrong when he proceeds: "What is the result? Vast riddles."
In writers for whom the polarity purity/impurity is dominant and all
consuming—Dostoevsky, Coetzee—moral dilemma is expressed with
great intellectual clarity, even when there is maximum emotional
confusion. Such writers do not resort to word games, or certainly not
for the main *feeling* of the text. It is the desire to have the upper hand
that creates a style as challenging as Joyce's, and this has nothing
to do with a "monstrous system of contradictions" coming out of
Catholicism.

Wells mentions power, its increase and concentration as a process
that is interesting to him. At this point it might occur to us that Wells,
an extremely ambitious man and, incidentally, one obsessed with
notching up as many sexual conquests as possible, is himself, like
Joyce, most concerned with the criterion of success, of affirming himself. Coming at the letter this way, we can see he rejects Joyce not
because he doesn't understand, but because he understands all too
well what is being asked of him. He will not give Joyce the satisfaction
of doing favours for him. In this case we could say that we have men
from radically different cultural backgrounds, but where the dominant semantic polarity in which they have grown up, winning/losing,
is nevertheless the same. Joyce, for family and cultural reasons, has
assumed a complex position in that semantic polarity, a position where
he sees himself as both winner and loser; he has to seem a victim in
order to assert his genius. Wells has no such problem. He simply has
to win and dominate. And this of course is why he writes such a long
letter. There was no need to say all this just to tell Joyce that he wasn't
planning to help promote *Work in Progress*. But, like Jung, Wells has to
get his digs in—"my mind has never been shocked to outcries by the
existence of water closets and menstrual bandages"—digs that establish, at least as he sees it, a certain superiority, a greater maturity. This,
as we saw, is one of the responses Joyce tends to prompt. Wells mentions another, "[your work] has its believers, its following," suggesting
that he understands perfectly the kind of master/disciple hierarchy
that imposes itself between writers like Joyce and readers who succumb to their seduction.

I shall not try to back up this reading of Wells's reaction in detail.
I offer the hypothesis simply to show that when I talk of a writer
being in the thrall to this or that polarity of value, I do not mean that

his work need necessarily be "similar" to that of another author for whom the polarity is equally important—there are so many factors involved—only that if we grasp the dominant polarity and its importance, much else will become clear. We will have a better sense of the values that really matter and generate emotion in the text, a clearer awareness of what is at stake.

My own resistance to Joyce arises from quite different energies than those that animate Wells. I feel inclined, almost compelled to argue that there are miserable moral implications in Joyce's work and that its effects on a reader could be noxious. I am aware how deeply unpopular it might be to say something like this in public, since the present world, so obsessed with morality when it comes to human rights, gender equality, paedophilia, etc., is eager to place aesthetics above and beyond morality (so that the Gerty MacDowell scene, which one could well imagine causing outcry and ministerial resignation if the masturbator were a politician caught on some observer's iPhone, is celebrated as charming). As a result, I resist my own instinct to criticize Joyce on moral grounds and do my masochistic best to admire what is obviously admirable in his work. And I really *do* admire it. Nevertheless, my aversion remains. I feel that to fall into thrall of Joyce is not simply to come out the loser in a confrontation, as Wells feels, but to risk *contamination*. This may seem rich coming from the man who wrote *Cara Massimina*. But *Cara Massimina* is precisely about the joys and dangers of contamination. It accepts the *existence* of contamination. It talks about it. For Joyce such sentiments are adolescent weakness. He would think me childish.

But what of my other readings? Imagine I am coming to a writer whose work lies under the enchantment of fear and courage, dependence and independence. The Norwegian Per Petterson, say. Petterson's hugely successful book *Out Stealing Horses* opens with a description of titmice banging into the window of the narrator's remote cabin home and falling dizzily into the evening snow. Warm inside, the ageing Trond Sander remarks, "I don't know what they want that I have."[1] The natural world is understood as an enigma, possibly a threat. Collisions, deaths, and bitter cold are the norm. A good cabin offering protection against the elements is essential. There is a great deal of weather in Petterson's stories and it is always beautiful and gruelling. Women are likewise beautiful and dangerous, for men. And men for women. The reader understands from page one that catastrophe will occur, and it will occur in part because the world—life—is so beautiful, it draws us powerfully to an ideal of bliss which is then promptly denied. The protagonist will be betrayed, crushed. That is always clear. The betrayal is not of the kind Joyce feared, not the betrayal of the friend who is also a rival and competitor. It is the abandonment of the person who should have been protecting you. A father, an older brother. These careless guardians drink heavily or fall in love elsewhere, or simply get sick and die, when they should be thinking of you and looking after you. Or worse still they approach you sexually when they shouldn't be doing that. Your only possible response to such menace is caution, expertise, resilience, stoicism. Petterson's heroes are always competent. They know how to cut wood, how to make cabins, how to swim, how to build fires. They also love to escape into a world of reading or contemplation. A world safe from immediate danger. They love libraries. Slowly we understand (the novel *It's Fine by Me* makes this explicit) how the act of writing combines the worlds of competence and evasion. The sentences are constructed with the same care that one builds a log cabin. The prose is a place of refuge. Thus in one way or another Petterson's protagonists protect themselves in a world full of beauty and danger. But in the end they are overwhelmed. They fall victim. It had to happen.

The only thing I know about Per Petterson's life, from an interview read years ago, is that his mother, father, and brother were killed in a ferry disaster, but this was when the author was already an adult, his personality long formed. In an interview with *The Guardian* he describes his father as "an athlete, looking like Tarzan"[2]—a strong man—and remarks, writing of himself in the third person, that "From the age of eighteen, he always wanted to become a writer, but for many years didn't dare to try because he was certain that he would fail."[3] He worked as a labourer, then as a librarian. Shortly before the ferry disaster, Petterson's mother had read his first novel and commented: "Well, I hope the next one won't be that childish." It was "a blow," Petterson remarks (*Guardian*). So apparently it is important for him to be "adult." Or it is important that his mother grant him this status. He comments: "I've thought a lot about what she said. I've tried to figure out what she meant. She was a little harsh, because she herself had survived so many things. She probably meant that I hadn't been ambitious enough in that novel, that I should go further. OK, you want to be a writer—be a writer then!" (*Guardian*) Petterson thinks his mother was telling him he wasn't risking enough. He was afraid.

In the same interview Petterson speaks of his difficulty sometimes facing author tours: Speaking of one trip he cancelled, he says: "I said I was ill—which wasn't untrue. I was invaded." It's a surprising word to use. He has devised a method, Petterson then explains, for coping with the stress of dealing with the public. He pretends he is "an actor playing Per Petterson." Again he confesses that ten people listening in the nearby village would make him more nervous than an audience of 600 in Manhattan, "because you would get a reprisal at the local shop next day. I get it whenever I've been on television. They talk about me, I know they do" (*Guardian*).

These are a few small facts gleaned from two or three hundred words of text that Petterson chose to put on a website and state in interview; yet they all have to do in one way or another with strength and weakness, fear and courage, being childish (dependent?) and grown up (independent?), being resourceful in the face of predicament. They entirely match the atmosphere we find in his books.

How does Tim Parks respond to this? Petterson is clearly a competent, indeed excellent writer. Very quickly, you're pulled into a world of trepidation. Life, as he describes it, is sufficiently seductive and attractive for you to believe in the anxiety it creates for his heroes. I enjoy and admire these books. But beyond the immediate suspense of the story and the pleasure in its unfolding and in the fine descriptions of landscape and character, the stories are not important for me. I don't feel I have to read them or that I can't put them down. His protagonists are charming victims, but no more than that. Or not for me. Again in the *Guardian* interview Petterson says of Arvid Jansen, who is a protagonist in many of the novels and who in *The Wake* undergoes the loss of his family in exactly the manner that Petterson lost his: "He's not my alter ego, he's my stunt man. Things happen to him that could have happened to me, but didn't. He has my mentality." Perhaps it is this aspect, this sense that Petterson's protagonists are simply waiting for the kinds of accidents Petterson fears, lightning conductors to draw off eventual calamity, that in the end isn't interesting to me. There is no moral tension in the books, nothing that really takes me to the core of the world *I* move in. But let me stress: I do not think my world is superior, it is just *my* world. I understand Petterson's popularity far more easily than I understand the continuing adulation of Joyce. I would rather read Petterson's *Wake* than Joyce's.

Peter Stamm, another writer who moves in a world of fear and apprehension, is rather different. His characters rarely face bad weather, though death and disease may constantly be on their minds. Whenever possible, they prefer their routines, their ruts. They don't expose themselves to the world until a need to be out and living simply forces them, albeit reluctantly, to get moving. Then they immediately fear attachment, they fear losing their independence, however arid that independence may be. They seek protection perhaps, but fear that it will trap them. Constantly drawn to sexual experience, they are quick to escape any consequences. Here is Andreas in *On a Day Like This*:

> Andreas spent his spring break in Normandy. Once again, he had intended to read Proust, but he ended up sitting around in the hotel, watching TV or reading the newspapers and maga-zines he bought at the station newsstand every morning. He spent a night with an unmarried woman teacher he had met on one of his long walks along the beach. He had been fascinated by her large breasts, and invited her to supper. It took a lot of effort to talk her into going up to his room, and then they talked for a lot longer while they emptied the minibar. While they made love, the woman kept moaning his name out loud, which got on his nerves. He was glad to be alone when he woke up late the following morning. She had left him a note, which he glanced at briefly before balling it up and throwing it away.[4]

It is hearing his name repeated by a lover that disturbs Andreas. Such a woman might make demands. What fascinates me is his (and Stamm's!) ruthlessness. He will not allow any moral dilemma, never mind any nicety to get in the way of his assertion of independence. Again and again Stamm sets up what in my world would be moral issues, but which then dissolve as morality is trumped by the fear of entrapment, the need for independence. In *Seven Years* Alexander, a young architect from lowly background, marries the beautiful but frigid Sonia, another architect, more confident in her intellectual background. Sonia is interested in success, fears anything that might get in her way, and Alexander seems like he might be the right, safe partner to add something to her career. Alexander finds Sonia "intimidating."[5] What he seeks in a building, he tells her, is "a place of refuge...protection from the elements" (p. 93). In that case he might as well live in "the nearest cave" she says (p. 94). She wants to build buildings whose spaces and shapes increase people's efficiency. The pair's uneasy love-making produces no offspring.

But Alexander has a secret. Before Sonia he met Ivona, a very plain Polish girl working in a religious bookshop, "docile" and "longsuffering" (p. 13). He finds her "disagreeable" (p. 13), but she falls in love with him, asks nothing of him, wants no one but him, never imposes on him, never contacts him but always waits for him. This simple, unthreatening acceptance, her open arms in a cluttered room (described very much as a cave) excites Alexander beyond all reason. He feels protected here. Nothing is demanded of him. Ivona falls pregnant.

It's precisely the situation that in a Tim Parks novel would force moral dilemma to its climax. There would be a showdown. There would be weeping and gnashing of teeth, guilt. Stamm doesn't do that. Very occasionally he does put a religious person in his novels, but these figures are caricatures, people Stamm knows exist but cannot understand or take seriously. Such is Ivona's landlord who contacts Alexander to tell him about his mistress's pregnancy. Attempting to stir up some guilt, he reminds Alexander of the biblical story of Jacob and Rachel.

> She loves you, he said, and sighed deeply. I shrugged my shoulders. With all her heart, he added. She's waited for you for seven years, the way Jacob waited for Rachel. I only vaguely remembered the story, but I remembered that at the end of seven years, Jacob had gone off with the wrong woman. Leah, Hartmeier said. And then he had to wait another seven years. I didn't understand what he was driving at...But the Lord saw that Leah was less beloved, and he opened her womb, said Hartmeier, and then I understood...He didn't speak, and it was as though I caught a glimpse of secret triumph in his face....
>
> Ivona is pregnant, said Hartmeier. (p. 154)

Of course the Bible story is comically inappropriate to describe the relationship between Alexander and Ivona and the attempt to align the two narratives creates much confusion, both in Alexander's mind and the reader's, rather as if Stamm were using this failed analogy to suggest how alien the moral position is to the people in his world.

When Stamm's characters finally meet the disasters they constantly fear and foresee, their reaction, paradoxically, is relief. The doubleness of their lives, the tension between seeking intensity and fearing it, desiring refuge but finding it limiting, is wearisome, taxing. Now they can be like men who go "freely to their graves to protect themselves from death" (p. 70). On hearing Hartmeier's news of Ivona's pregnancy Alexander "felt a great feeling of calm and a kind of relief. I would have to talk to Sonia" (p. 154).

In the world of Tim Parks such a reaction would be hard to imagine. Perhaps a character of mine could behave like this, but he would not be the main character, and his relief would be short-lived, as indeed, reading *Seven Years*, I expected Alexander's would be. Indeed I still remember my fascination as Stamm leads his hero to the showdown with the intimidating Sonia—he really does make us feel how daunting such a woman can be—and again the inevitable confrontation, with the frighteningly vulnerable Ivona. Now the shit will hit the fan, I was thinking, gripped. Now someone will have to face up to the reality of who he is.

Nothing of the kind. Stamm's characters don't do showdowns. They are afraid of drama. They think only of their own needs and safety. Sonia proposes that she take Ivona's baby herself. It will save her the animal trouble of pregnancy. She can become a mother without any biological bother to get in the way of her career. Reassured that his marriage can be saved, Alexander agrees. Ivona doesn't resist. She surrenders her child without protest and continues to be utterly submissive to Alexander's requirements. So the story can go on more perversely than before with the brilliant, sterile wife bringing up the child of the dumb but fertile mistress. Nobody experiences guilt or moral dilemma.

Perhaps what I am saying, what I am discovering, as I talk through my different reaction to these two authors, is that when, albeit recognizing another criterion as dominant—in this case fear, the need for protection, the contrasting desire for courage and independence—an author nevertheless creates situations that I read as moral issues, then I can go beyond merely admiring the writing and become fascinated by the story. And what fascinates me is this convincing representation of people who move in a completely different atmosphere from the one I move in. Instead, when no moral issue is involved, as in Petterson, or in some of Stamm's short stories, that is, when it is not a case of the fear semantic trumping the moral semantic, but merely a question of anxiety and survival, I am less interested, however well written the book may be.

Again, let me be quite clear: it is not that I think writing *has to* be about moral issues; nor that I want to insist that the situation that Stamm describes need necessarily be such an issue. It is simply that this is the kind of situation that would most arouse the tension between self indulgence and self sacrifice that I grew up in. It's a story that alerts me to who I am and the position I would take in these circumstances. To see someone else negotiate a situation like this without remotely experiencing it as moral is intriguing. It might even be therapeutic, if only Stamm didn't present his characters as so inadequate. For here we have to add a point that has so far gone unnoticed. Stamm's characters themselves sense that this situation *should* cause moral crisis; the fact that it doesn't confirms for them their sense of their own emptiness. They don't enjoy their ability not to fall into a state of moral confusion; it is not an achievement for them to have gone beyond the moral, as it might be for a hero of mine, for Morris Duckworth, say. They simply allow their lives to be governed by fear, fear of the consequences if they act differently from the way they do, not fear of guilt, or a loss of identity for not having behaved "properly."

In J. M. Coetzee's *Disgrace* David Lurie, professor at Cape Town University, where Coetzee himself taught, satisfies his fifty-year-old libido seeing a prostitute once a week, a girl provided by an upmarket escort agency. After two marriages he no longer wishes to tie the conjugal knot. On the other hand he has conjugal feelings for his escort girl. He brings her presents, takes and gives affection. This allows him to feel he is not exploiting her. He may not be a good man but he is not a bad man; he has generous tendencies. Good and bad is the dominant force field, within which, for the moment, David has found a precarious balance.

However, very soon he sees his woman in the street with her children, away from the upmarket apartment where they meet. This makes him aware of the drama of her life. She has sex with him to bring up her children. After this contact she refuses to see him again, refuses to recognize him when he phones her. In short, she breaks down his cosy version of their liaison and forces him to acknowledge that the relationship was one of exploitation, prostitution.

David now has an affair with a student following his lecture course. The moral dilemma is stepped up. He doesn't molest or importune the girl in any way. She is an adult and a free agent. He gives her every opportunity to say no. There is nothing *illegal* in what he has done. On the other hand he is in a relationship of power in her regard, even if he has no intention of using that power to manipulate her. Her boyfriend discovers the relationship, blocks it. Feeling he has certain rights and needs in the girl's regard, David oversteps the mark and tries, briefly, to force himself on her. The girl withdraws from his teaching course and he is denounced at the university. A professor's nightmare.

In what follows fear and courage are present but never determining. All kinds of considerations regarding belonging are also involved, since the student and the professor come from different sides of the black/white divide and different religions. Her family are Jewish. The question of whether David is a winner or a loser is likewise to the fore. He is a successful man up to a point, but in post-apartheid South Africa his talents of literary analysis are no longer required and his deeper ambitions to write literature seem more remote than ever.

None of these values, however, create the determining issue for David and Coetzee. What matters is, is he a good man, or not? David goes before the university tribunal set up to judge him and refuses to accept their definition of good and evil. His relationships with women are positive, he insists, they enrich him and them. He will not make a pro forma apology. For him morality, his dignity as a moral agent, is too important for him to subscribe to these games of political convenience.

We are now, or at least I am now, in that zone where a writer says, I could/should have written this myself. Not in a sense of rivalry with Coetzee, or comparison of talents. His are huge. But because this story is my territory. There is not a shred of an enigmatic episode here for me, not a moment of surprise. All is terribly full of exactly the meaning I would give the story. Hence the pleasures are very different from those I derive from reading Stamm. In fact pleasure is hardly the word. I am riveted.

David now goes to stay with his daughter in the country. She also believes strongly in being good; she is her father's daughter. But her sense of goodness has to do with accepting a new black-governed Africa, accepting responsibility for the sins of her fathers, the sins of the whites against the blacks. Belonging is present as a criterion for making decisions and acting; the daughter wants to belong to the new South Africa. But hierarchically good and evil are more important. Her decision to accept the new state of affairs in South Africa is the decision of someone who feels that this is the "good" way to belong. When she is brutally attacked and raped by three black men, she quickly accepts the calamity as a form of penitence. Her father cannot see it like that.

What is so fine about Coetzee's work is that he never makes it clear where he stands on the moral issues he repeatedly raises. The books intensify and feed the reader's awareness of moral dilemma, without orienting him in this or that direction. Strong emotions are expressed on all sides of various divides, but it's hard for the reader to establish a clear position, perhaps hard for Coetzee himself to take one. David, punished for his relationship with a student, cannot accept that his daughter's rapists not be pursued, condemned, punished. He cannot accept his daughter's decision to become part of the community that conceals and protects her rapists. A comparison is thus invited between David's misdemeanour with the student and this rape, but the two events seem incommensurate. Or at least they seem so to *me*, but not to others I have spoken to. I have had interesting, even heated discussions about this, most notably with James Meek on one long afternoon in Adelaide. Meek insisted that the events were crimes of the same order and I simply couldn't agree with that.

At a certain point in the story, David appears to change his position and to accept some kind of analogy between his affair with the girl and what happened to his daughter; he seeks out the student's parents, calls at their house and gets on his knees to beg their forgiveness. Having previously sympathized with the professor as he defended himself before a hypocritical tribunal (feeling at this point that Coetzee also was sympathizing), I am now in deep disagreement with him. It seems to me a mistake that David put himself on a par, morally, with men who have brutally assaulted and raped his daughter. Since the student did not in any way resist David's initial quiet seduction, to beg forgiveness of her parents suggests that this embrace, which has previously been described as enriching and even *necessary*, was on the contrary a heinous crime.

All the same, David's visit to his student's home is far from being an enigmatic episode for me. The desire to abase oneself, to confess to certain sins, *even if deep down one doesn't feel they are sins*, is an impulse I recognize all too well, instilled in me from earliest childhood. To confess is to be reassured that one has a moral dimension and is placing oneself on the good side of the good/evil divide. So here is the doubt that comes to my mind, when I read *Disgrace*: is David, and perhaps Coetzee, getting a fillip to his own self esteem from this, as I see it, unnecessary, self-indulgent, distastefully theatrical gesture of repentance? I simply cannot know. Coetzee gives us the episode and leaves the conundrum to us. Reading his laconic autobiographical trilogy, *Boyhood, Youth, Summertime*, it's soon clear that Coetzee occupies the position of he who doesn't want to be caught occupying any position at all. He enjoys the perplexity of his audience. All the same he does want to be thought of as morally engaged. He wants us to feel that these questions are urgent for him. When asked why he is a vegetarian, Coetzee dismisses all the standard reasons and talks about hoping he can save his soul.

What are we to make of the last pages of *Disgrace* where David struggles towards some kind of sainthood by working in the kennels for stray dogs, showing kindness and respect to them even as they are put down because there is no home for them in contemporary South Africa (again the idea of belonging, in relation to morality, goodness, pathos)? Even the art that David now tries to make, writing an opera about the sinful, sexually indulgent Byron, but sung to the melancholy twang of the banjo, has something theatrically penitential about it. Where making art might once have lifted someone above the good and evil polarity into the paradise of celebrity where the chosen ones like Joyce move in amoral bliss, here it is a castigated lament, with the further suggestion that the whole business of making art might seem to be a kind of sin, an extravagance that needs to be chastened, hence Coetzee's own spare style.

Even when I kick against it, *Disgrace* is a book that speaks so intensely to me that the reflection that it comes out of a distant culture, a distant land, a highly complex social and racial situation that I know next to nothing about is extraordinary. I have read the book four or five times, and taught it for some years in a seminar. It was fascinating to me to watch how the students divided into those who got it at once, I mean got it *the way I did*, and those for whom the book was simply a mystery, an enigmatic episode from start to finish, at best a rather lame thriller.

To sum up on reader reactions: I am suggesting that rather than following, or *only* following an aesthetics of narrative, an appreciation of prose style and the content and story structure it delivers, a large part of my response to a novel will depend on the critical semantic in the author's work, the values that are most keenly felt, and then again the position the author occupies in regard to those values. It's not that a novel written by someone like my mother, whose life lay very much under the enchantment of good and evil, would necessarily interest me, for her position in that atmosphere was absolutely stable and suffocatingly prescriptive. But someone who has difficulty in that world and knows how to convey that state of mind through narrative will immediately have an attraction for me that goes beyond any purely aesthetic achievement, to the point that, when speaking of written narrative, one really wonders if there is ever any sense in trying to separate aesthetics from content and values.

Writers moving in other worlds and expressing the endless positions that in different families and cultures each semantic allows, may also be absolutely fascinating for me, to the extent that they express themselves in ways and around situations that allow me to savour the distance between us. In the end, if one wants to recover, for the novel, some sense of an ethical and therapeutic value it is in the story's ability to allow us to feel how different people really are from each other, how different the atmospheres in which they move and the criteria that guide their behaviour. It is precisely when we intensely disagree with a book, or when we feel that a character is acting in a way that is quite incredible to us— Bloom's response to Molly's betrayal, for example—that we should begin to wonder whether this is mere incompetence (quite possible, of course) or whether it alerts us to a whole different way of conceiving of the world and positioning oneself in it.

Notes

1. Per Petterson, *Out Stealing Horses*, trans. Anne Born (London: Vintage, 2010), 1.
2. See <http://www.theguardian.com/culture/2009/jan/03/per-petterson-interview> Hereafter cited as "*Guardian*."
3. See <http://perpetterson.com/per-petterson-biography>.
4. Peter Stamm, *On a Day Like This*, trans. Michael Hofmann (New York: Other Press, 2007), 45.
5. Peter Stamm, *Seven Years*, trans. Michael Hofmann (New York: Other Press, 2010), 25.

6

Terrifying Bliss

Fear in the face of a world construed as dangerous and, at the
same time, the urge to be rid of protective anchors and refuges,
necessarily has a history behind it.

Valeria Ugazio, *Permitted and Forbidden Stories*, 83.

Let us now move away from my subjective position and offer a more
"neutral" analysis of the conflicting values at work in the writings of
Thomas Hardy and D. H. Lawrence. What I'll be trying to do here,
concentrating mainly on Hardy, but offering Lawrence as a foil, is to
show how for both the key emotion for determining action is fear.
With these two authors we have the rare advantage that Lawrence
wrote at length about Hardy in terms that suggest he had appreciated
both what they shared and where they differed, why they wrote about
the same issues, but produced such entirely different works.

Hardy was born more dead than alive in the small village of Bockhampton, Dorset, south-west England, on 2 June 1840, less than six
months after his parents married. His father, a small-time builder,
named the boy Thomas after both himself and his own father, giving
no second name to distinguish the newborn. He was just another gen-
eration. His mother, Jemima, a servant and cook, had reached the
relatively mature age of 26 without marrying, had had no desire to do
so before this unwanted pregnancy, and would always warn her children against the move. Jemima's own mother had married in the last
month of a pregnancy (her second) and brought up seven children in
extreme poverty. Jemima would have three more after Thomas.

Frail, not expected to survive, Hardy was kept at home till age 8,
learning to read and play the fiddle from his parents. Throughout
her long life his mother would always refer to him as "her rather
delicate 'boy' "[1] while in his memoirs Hardy recalls that when asked

what he wished to do as a grown-up he would protest that "he did not want at all to be a man, or to possess things, but to remain as he was, in the same spot, and to know no more people than he already knew" (Tomalin, 24). "If only he could prevent himself growing up!" thinks Jude, in *Jude the Obscure*, "He did not want to be a man!"[2] All Hardy's major novels present us with a child, or childish adult, who is, as it were, thrust out into the world before he or she is ready for experience. As late as 1917 Hardy was still describing himself at his first school as an unfledged bird, "Pink, tiny, crisp-curled" (Tomalin, 323).

When the young Hardy was eventually sent to school he did well and as a result was articled to an architect in Dorchester at 16. Receiving his first salary at 20, he was now able to live independently from his family, though he always returned home to mother at the weekends. In 1862, however, aged 22, Hardy took the bold decision to go to London to pursue an architect's career. Living far away from his family, he won two prizes with the firm he worked for and seemed set for a bright future when, in 1867, he abandoned London for home, pleading on the one hand ill health (there was no specific pathology) and on the other the impossibility of "pushing his way into [the] influential sets"[3] that could give him work as an architect. Whether this was really such an obstacle is hard to say. In any event, what saved the retreat to Dorset from feeling like complete failure was that Hardy brought back with him four hundred pages of a novel in progress. Resuming part-time architect's work in Dorchester, he settled down to completing his book at home. Mother's protection in Bockhampton was combined with aspirations that would be fulfilled in the big city.

In the event, this first novel, *The Poor Man and the Lady*, was never published. Most critics speak of it as being rejected for publication by an obtuse literary establishment;[4] however, in the version of events Hardy offered in his posthumously published autobiography, the publisher Chapman did accept the novel for publication, requiring the author to deposit £20 to cover eventual losses. Hardy agreed but was then warned by Chapman's reader, George Meredith, that the inflammatory nature of the novel would provoke controversy and might compromise his reputation. Hardy withdrew the book.

In what way was *The Poor Man and the Lady* "inflammatory"? Later in life Hardy claimed, extraordinarily, that the novel had been his "most original" work, "a sweeping dramatic satire of the squirearchy and nobility, London society, the vulgarity of the middle class, modern Christianity, church restoration and political and domestic morals in general...the tendency of the writing being socialistic, not to say revolutionary" (see T & F, 62). Here originality and courage seem to be superimposed. Hardy, who lived a very conservative life, is claiming in old age that he had been revolutionary, once.

The story in the novel again had to do with courage. The main character, Will Strong, "was the son of peasants...showed remarkable talent at the village school, and was...educated as a draughtsman...". In love with the daughter of a local squire and rejected because of his humble background, he ended up being "sent up to London, where he was taken into the office of an eminent architect and made striking progress."[5] At this point the story became that of "an isolated student cast upon the billows of London with no protection but his brains" (Tomalin, 64).

Aside from fear and courage, other polarities are in evidence in *The Poor Man and the Lady*. The book's title announces a class conflict tangled with sexual attraction and offering the contrasts wealth/poverty and simplicity/sophistication, which prepare us for the polarity justice/injustice when Will is forbidden to court his lady because he is poor. It is out of a consequent "pique" (Gosse, 215) that in London Will takes up radical politics (something Hardy never did), militancy being thus presented as subordinate or secondary to romantic gratification and possibly rash, the negative or at least dangerous side of courage.

However, Hardy knew where he stood on social injustice. His position was stable there. More problematic was how to respond to it, what risks should be run to redress injustice. In the case of *The Poor Man and the Lady* one might say that Hardy had been braver in the story he told than he chose to be in reality; or rather, fiction and the real world were not so separate as he hoped. A book is a real event; you cannot write enthusiastically about a Will Strong taking on the establishment if you are not strong-willed enough to take on the establishment yourself by publishing it.

His novel unpublished, Hardy could once again present his failure as a provincial boy's difficulty "pushing his way into influential sets" and this is how it continues to be talked about in most Hardy criticism.

However only the following year, aged 31, Hardy would publish his first, now entirely innocuous novel, *Desperate Remedies* (the title of this rustic comedy speaks worlds), with a London publisher, then his second, *Under the Greenwood Tree*, at 32, at which point, with a contract signed to write a third, this time for more lucrative serialization, Hardy was already able to dedicate himself entirely to writing. Even today such an achievement would be remarkable. The literary establishment was not after all so hostile to a country boy.

I offer all this to suggest how ambiguous, in Hardy's mature novels, is the relationship between social criticism and the misfortunes and defeats of his characters: snobbery, injustice, discrimination there may be, but these obstacles can also offer the insecure child-adult a ready excuse to give up and go back home, or they may confirm a preconception that life away from the parental hearth is unspeakably dangerous. Alternatively, we could say that, avoiding Will Strong's mistake of making radical decisions out of pique and playing instead the card of the provincial author who can write charmingly about rural foibles and beautiful landscapes, Hardy had managed to break through London's resistance and get his foot in the door. In letters to publishers at this time he stressed that what he most cared about was reaching the widest possible audience, to the point of actually inviting any "censorship" that would help him achieve this. We are a million miles from the mentality of Joyce.

In 1874 Hardy published *Far from the Madding Crowd*, his first major success and the first of the novels for which he is remembered today. Essentially the work reads like an extended and precarious betrothal. The reader knows more or less from the start which two characters should marry and live happily ever after, but the author introduces every kind of obstacle and impediment to keep us on the edge of our seats. The movement and trajectory of the story encourages a pleasurable anxiety.

Pragmatic, independent, solid shepherd, Gabriel Oak, proposes to orphan girl Bathsheba (named after a supreme object of desire). Bold and beautiful, she rejects him, but not outright. He loses his entire flock and livelihood in an accident for which he is not responsible and becomes poor. She becomes rich inheriting a farm from an uncle; he finds work on her farm. So far, all is coincidence. Socially above Gabriel now, Bathsheba unwisely attracts the attention of proud local landowner Boldwood, who bullies her toward marriage. This would be another upward move, socially. Courageous in running her farm, Bathsheba is a child when it comes to romance. Before she can succumb to Boldwood, the disreputable but dashing Sergeant Troy seduces her with a dazzling display of swordsmanship that involves having his blade flash all around her body as she stands frightened and adoring. The passage is one of Hardy's finest, fusing fear and desire. Here is an extract. Watch the three polarities, winning/losing, fear/courage, and finally good/evil, all intertwine as Troy passes from innocuous preliminaries to his terrifying seduction act (words that fall into these polarities are flagged in bold type).

"You are my **antagonist**, with this difference from real **warfare**, that I shall miss you every time by one hair's breadth, or perhaps two. Mind you don't **flinch**, whatever you do."

"I'll be sure not to!" she said **invincibly**....

He pointed to about a yard in front of him.

Bathsheba's **adventurous** spirit was beginning to find some grains of relish in these highly novel proceedings. She took up her position as directed, **facing** Troy.

"Now just to learn whether you have **pluck** enough to let me do what I wish, I'll give you a preliminary test."

He flourished the sword...and the next thing of which she was conscious was that the point and blade of the sword were darting with a gleam towards her left side, just above her hip; then of their reappearance on her right side, emerging as it were from between her ribs, having apparently passed through her body. The third item of consciousness was that of seeing the same sword, perfectly clean and free from blood held vertically in Troy's hand...

"Oh!" she cried out in **affright**, pressing her hand to her side. "Have you run me through?—no, you have not! Whatever have you done!"

"I have not touched you," said Troy, quietly. "It was mere sleight of hand. The sword passed behind you. Now you are not **afraid**, are you? Because if you are I can't perform. I give my word that I will not only not hurt you, but not once touch you."

"I don't think I am **afraid**. You are quite sure you will not hurt me?"

"Quite sure."

"Is the sword very sharp?"

"O no—only stand as still as a statue. Now!"

In an instant the atmosphere was transformed to Bathsheba's eyes. Beams of light caught from the low sun's rays, above, around, in front of her, well-nigh shut out earth and heaven— all emitted in the marvellous evolutions of Troy's reflecting blade, which seemed everywhere at once, and yet nowhere specially. These circling gleams were accompanied by a keen rush that was almost a whistling—also springing from all sides of her at once. In short, she was enclosed in a firmament of light, and of sharp hisses, resembling a sky-full of meteors close at hand...

"That outer loose lock of hair wants tidying," he said, before she had moved or spoken. "Wait: I'll do it for you."

An arc of silver shone on her right side: the sword had descended. The lock dropped to the ground.

"**Bravely** borne!" said Troy. "You didn't **flinch** a shade's thickness. **Wonderful in a woman!**"

"It was because I didn't expect it. O, you have spoilt my hair!"

"Only once more."

"No—no! I am **afraid** of you—indeed I am!" she cried....

[At this point Troy kills a caterpillar on her bodice with the tip of his sword.]

"But how could you chop off a curl of my hair with a sword that has no edge?"

"No edge! This sword will shave like a razor...."...

Bathsheba, **overcome by a hundred tumultuous feelings** resulting from the scene, abstractedly sat down on a tuft of heather....

She felt **powerless to withstand or deny him. He was altogether too much for her....** He drew near and said, "I must be leaving you."

He drew nearer still. A minute later and she saw his scarlet form disappear amid the ferny thicket, almost in a flash, like a brand swiftly waved.

That minute's interval had brought the blood beating into her face, set her stinging as if aflame to the very hollows of her feet, and **enlarged emotion to a compass which quite swamped thought**. It had brought upon her a stroke resulting, as did that of **Moses in Horeb**, in a liquid stream—here a stream of tears. She felt like one who has **sinned a great sin**.

The circumstance had been the gentle dip of Troy's mouth downwards upon her own. He had kissed her.[6]

Troy presents the encounter as a duel with two antagonists, and though in military terms it is a mock duel, in romantic terms it is real enough and there is no doubt as to who is the winner: though Bathsheba is "adventurous" and believes herself "invincible," Troy's sword creates an enchantment of movement and light that isolates her and "well-nigh shut out earth and heaven." "Enclosed" by his performance, she is overcome by tumultuous feelings, "powerless to withstand"; he is "too much" for her.

What are these feelings that overcome her? She says she isn't "afraid," she doesn't "flinch," but then she tells him this is only because she didn't understand the danger. Realizing how sharp the blade is and how close to death she has been, retrospective fear has her swooning. One has the impression that for Bathsheba fear and desire are inextricable. She is not concerned, as he is, about winning or losing, nor does she even begin to frame the experience morally. She is overwhelmed by the excitement.

At the climax of the passage, we have a rather odd ellipsis: Troy draws near her, then nearer, and the next thing we know he has gone, like the flashing of a brand; suddenly we have an abrupt shift of register with a portentous, perhaps slightly comic, reference to the Bible; in Horeb, Moses, who had been told to speak to the rock in order to obtain life-giving water, struck it instead in a moment of frustration, or pique, in any event rashly. God gave him the water He had promised, but for his sin of disobedience, punished him by denying him entry to the Promised Land. Bathsheba's sudden tears—a mystery to the reader at this point—are likened to that gushing of water from the rock. But what on earth has happened to justify such an analogy? Bathsheba feels that "she has sinned a great sin." This would align her with Moses. She is appalled. Only now do we learn that in that brief ellipsis Troy has kissed her.

The effect of the narrative is to suggest that something fatal has happened in the moral plane, catching ourselves and Bathsheba by surprise. We were bamboozled by excitement and fear as Troy flourished his sword. Nobody felt they were being tempted, no one experienced the idea of sin. In this sense the analogy (like Stamm's "seven years" analogy) is wildly inappropriate. Angry with God, Moses struck the rock; here instead emotion "had brought upon her a stroke"—that is, Bathsheba is the rock that is struck (by Troy?) and produces water, tears. Appearing to raise Bathsheba's great sin to biblical importance, the analogy seems too tenuous and inflated to hold: surely it's incongruous for us to think of Bathsheba as sinning a great sin like Moses did. And in fact the reader is very far from thinking that. Yet Bathsheba is appalled. She understands sin not on the moral plane of someone who is first tempted, then indulges, then repents, but from the point of view of someone afraid that she has been induced to make a huge mistake for which others will condemn her. Public morality is just one more thing that can cause anxiety. It is out of the fear, we later learn, that following this kiss her reputation has been compromised, that Bathsheba hastily marries Troy.

The sudden marriage to Troy leaves the reader aghast. The novel didn't feel like it was going to be an unhappy book. And in the end it isn't. Though marriage for the Victorians was very much "till death us do part," Bathsheba is to get the benefit of a swift parting. Exposed as a rake for his behaviour with another woman, Troy is murdered by his rival Boldwood. With both pretenders removed at a stroke (since Boldwood must go to prison), humble, hard-working Gabriel, who has done everything to protect Bathsheba and her farm during a terrifying storm, can finally claim his prize.

To recapitulate: the whole story is a space of excited trepidation between a proposal of marriage and its consummation. The main emotion the reader experiences is anxiety that things will not work out as he feels they should, then pleasure when they do. Bathsheba makes *mistakes*, because she is sensitive to life's extraordinary power to enchant and seduce, but she is not *immoral*.

What were the events in Hardy's life in the years immediately before he told this tale? Remaining in Dorset, after the rejection of *The Poor Man and the Lady*, he had been trying to decide whether the future lay in architecture or writing, preferring writing but despairing of making a living that way. Understandably, he was looking for a mate, but anxious about finding the right woman. In 1865 he complains to his notebook: "There is not that regular gradation among womankind that there is among men. You may meet with 999 exactly alike, and then the thousandth—not a little better, but far above them. Practically therefore it is useless for a man to seek after this thousandth to make her his" (T & F, 49).

What to do, then? The danger was that one would fall for the wrong person. In 1868, writing of an attractive woman seen during a boat trip to Lulworth, he remarks: "Saw her for the last time standing on deck as the boat moved off. White feather in hat, brown dress, Dorset dialect, Classic features, short upper lip. A woman I wd have married offhand, with probably disastrous results."[7] Desire triggers the inhibiting notion of the fatal mistake, the kind of mistake Bathsheba makes with Troy. This is what Hardy is afraid of. Then it happens.

In March 1870 a Dorset architect sent Hardy to Cornwall to assess the condition of a church in the tiny hamlet of St Juliot and here he fell in love with Emma Gifford, sister-in-law of the incumbent clergyman. Emma was interested in literature and she was a bold horsewoman. "She was so *living*," Hardy felt (T & F, 74). In a poem written that same year Cornwall is renamed Lyonesse, a land of legend:

> When I set out for Lyonesse
> A hundred miles away,
> The rime was on the spray,
> And starlight lit my lonesomeness,
> When I set out for Lyonesse
> A hundred miles away.
>
> What would bechance at Lyonesse
> While I should sojourn there
> No prophet durst declare,
> Nor did the wisest wizard guess
> What would bechance at Lyonesse
> While I should sojourn there
>
> When I came back from Lyonesse
> With magic in my eyes,

> All marked with mute surmise
> My radiance rare and fathomless,
> When I came back from Lyonnesse
> With magic in my eyes!
>   (*Hardy Poems*, 254)

As with Bathsheba's first kiss, we have a before and an after, with—
elided in the middle—an experience that transforms someone absolutely and irreversibly, something that cannot be spoken. In this case
the transformation is positive. But again it is something over which
one has no control, and so, in a sense, fatal, frightening.

In love, Hardy did not hurry to marriage. His mother was against
it. Emma was a middle-class woman, hence marriage to her would
complete Hardy's move away from his kinfolk. She was also penniless.
It was the worst of both worlds. Emma's father was against her marrying into a lower class. In short, there was good reason for being
cautious and enjoying an exciting romantic correspondence which
Hardy later compared to that between Robert Browning and Elizabeth Barrett, though those two of course had thrown caution to the
winds and very romantically eloped. In the end Hardy waited four
years; both he and Emma would be 34 when they married. It was late
for a woman in those times. One thing immensely in Emma's favour
during this period was that when Hardy spoke of giving up writing,
she always insisted he take the courageous decision and follow his
vocation. She was reinforcing his impulse toward independence and
freedom. One thing Hardy would always grant Emma was that she
had courage. It was the decisive quality.

Far from the Madding Crowd was written in this period of heady trepidation, anxiously prospecting the fatal moment when he would go
against his mother's will, join himself with another woman and
change his life forever. All the biographies attest that it was the happi-
est time of his life; everything was potential, nothing yet spoiled in
realization. Again and again in his forthcoming novels, which are
above all stories of attempted and failed partnerships, one partner will
prefer "perpetual betrothal"[8] to consummation.

As it turned out, the marriage of Bathsheba and Gabriel, as it came
from Hardy's pen, preceded his own marriage to Emma by a matter
of weeks. Both ceremonies were carried out in great secrecy, in Bathsheba's case because of the scandal surrounding her first marriage, in

Hardy's because he always did everything possible to avoid the public eye and eventual criticism.

Published in 1878, most critics agree that *The Return of the Native* is the first of Hardy's more daring and characteristic works. And it is characteristic above all in this, that after some initial scene-setting offering every kind of easy pleasure—quaint characterization, lush landscape description, plenty of intriguing plot anticipation—the narrative becomes extremely painful to read, so consistently and inexorably do the characters, singly and collectively, engineer their own unhappiness.

In this regard, there is a moment midway through the novel where the main character, Clym, already deeply troubled by his mother's mysterious death, goes out of his way to find a little boy who may be able to tell him exactly what happened to her. When he asks the boy's mother for permission to speak to the child, she "regarded [Clym] in a peculiar and criticizing manner. To anybody but a half-blind man it would have said, 'You want another of the knocks which have already laid you so low.'" As the boy then tells his tale, stringing together facts that will destroy Clym's life, the same woman "looked as if she wondered how a man could want more of what had stung him so deeply" (*Native*, 5.2). At this point many readers may realize that the same thought is on their minds too: why am I persevering with a novel so painful that every turn of the page seems to require an act of courage?

The novel is set on Egdon Heath, fictional name for a desolate area near Dorchester in Hardy's imagined, parallel world of Wessex. A "vast tract of unenclosed wild," infertile and intractable, its community left behind by nineteenth-century progress, without even a church, "the Egdon waste" is at once overwhelmingly real and a place of the mind, a landscape of ancient burial mounds and prehistoric remains, "unaltered as the stars" (*Native*, 1.1), subject to the most intemperate weather, seething with plant and insect life of the most resilient and unprepossessing varieties. Anyone who wants to make anything of himself or herself in the modern world, anyone who wishes to be independent and free, *must* leave Egdon. But as our title tells us, the novel is about someone who has come back.

Against this all-conditioning backdrop, the novel presents six characters who, in seeking to lift themselves above it, will contrive to make each other as miserable as people can be. The bland young orphan Thomasin, "a pleasing and innocent woman" (1.6), is timid and sensible in all things except her determination to marry the shifty Mr Wildeve, almost the only eligible bachelor on the heath. Wildeve is a qualified engineer who for reasons never explained has fallen back on running the heath's only inn and is looking to bring either security or excitement into his life through marriage. Thomasin would bring security; the more striking, passionate, raven-haired Eustacia, another orphan, living alone with her carelessly cantankerous grandfather, is infinitely more alluring; but her inflexible determination to leave the heath for a free and fashionable city life would require Wildeve to abandon his safe economic base and take a risk in the world.

Thomasin's cousin, Clym, is the native whose return to Egdon is so inexplicable to the others and above all to his widowed mother, Mrs Yeobright, who is also aunt and guardian to Thomasin. Clym has been working in the diamond business in Paris, at the very heart of modern fashion and culture, but having deemed this world superficial and unsatisfying he now wishes to set up a school for the poor people of Egdon; he thus returns to the heath in order to put others less advantaged than himself in a position to gain their independence and leave it.

Initially unhappy that her niece wants to marry a man whom she feels is unworthy, Mrs Yeobright is now appalled that her son should renounce his good fortune in Paris for a provincial philanthropy she finds entirely unconvincing. Middle-class and struggling to keep her family upwardly mobile, Mrs Yeobright is invariably correct in her assessment of Clym's and Thomasin's poor choices but fatally clumsy in her attempts to change their minds; every move she makes will be counterproductive, hastening the outcomes she fears. When Clym and Eustacia fall in love, so that the energies of he who is most determined to stay in Egdon and she who is most determined to leave now collide, the older woman's dismay knows no bounds.

To complete the odd picture there is the mysterious, quaintly named, Diggory Venn. Originally a dairy farmer, Venn once dared to ask for Thomasin's hand in marriage and was rebuffed, because not of the right class. Since then he has become a reddleman, an itinerant tradesman selling red dye to sheep farmers, with the result that he himself is stained permanently red by the materials he works with. Still set on Thomasin, combining resilience, ubiquity, and benevolent cunning, Venn contrives to be both frightening bogeyman and generous deus ex machina.

How on earth, you ask, could an experienced reader be deeply pained by the antics of such unpromising dramatis personae? "Our sympathies [are] never…strongly enlisted in any of the three [major characters]," complained one contemporary reviewer of Eustacia, Clym, and Wildeve (*Native*, 424). Another felt the book's disregard for realism reached levels "repugnant to our sense of the probable," the whole performance being "intensely artificial" (422). Indeed key moments in the novel seem contrived beyond belief, not just a belief in the events, but in Hardy's having wanted to make his manipulation of them so evident; there are a dozen points where the plot turns on a character's overhearing precisely the part of a conversation that will give the wrong impression and lead to calamity. The tragedy is "arbitrary and accidental," wrote one reviewer, the sadness "unnecessary and uncalled for," "mournful and cruel," so that all in all for those "who have the weakness of liking to be pleasantly interested in a book it is also very disagreeable" (421–2).

When critics quote first reviews of classic novels it is usually to suggest the naïvety of the initial response, the superiority of our own. Yet all these comments seem appropriate, all address those aspects of Hardy's later fiction that are unique and demand a response, if only because, for all the arbitrariness and disagreeableness, *The Return of the Native* is nevertheless riveting and actually *more* engaging and far more painful than the traditional variety of tragedy, featuring, as they taught us at school, a great and noble character whose fatal personality flaws make his or her downfall inevitable. Hardy doesn't have great and noble characters, yet the stories compel our attention.

As *The Return of the Native* opens Wildeve and Thomasin have gone to a neighbouring town to marry, but failed to do so because the certificate Wildeve had procured isn't valid there. Thomasin isn't convinced that the problem is merely one of the certificate and wonders about Wildeve's commitment. Feeling compromised and slighted, she now questions her own commitment. We discover that a previous attempt to marry was blocked when Mrs Yeobright intervened during the ceremony, claiming that she knew of an impediment to the union and thus humiliating both Wildeve and her niece. Initially, then, Mrs Yeobright must have allowed the marriage to go ahead, then changed her mind to prevent it, then changed her mind again to allow it to go ahead. A situation has been created where, whatever ultimately happens, there will be bad feeling on all sides.

Rather than repeating the complaint that Hardy's characters are not of the "great" variety necessary for "real" tragedy, it is more useful to turn the proposition on its head and say that if we did have "great" characters the Hardy kind of tragedy could not happen. Were Wildeve a more substantial figure he would either know his mind on Thomasin and sweep her off her feet, or he would leave her alone altogether. Were Thomasin "great" she would hardly be thrown into confusion by a bureaucratic hitch. Nor would a more forceful guardian vacillate as Mrs Yeobright does.

Eustacia and Clym are similarly uncertain. Eustacia has grown weary of Wildeve, but renews her interest when he turns to Thomasin; she then falls in love with the *idea* of Clym even before seeing him, simply because he has been living in Paris (freedom/independence); later she falls in love with the real Clym, but without renouncing the idea that he can be persuaded to return to Paris. Clym falls in love with Eustacia's unconventional character and beauty but immediately and most improbably imagines her as a charity school teacher, then is rather too concerned about his mother's hostile reaction and the effect of this emotional upheaval on his philanthropic projects. First deciding to delay the marriage, he then allows himself to be hurried into it, because anxious that Eustacia is anxious that he will allow his anxious mother to change his mind. Curiously, even the landscape with its tiny meandering pathways through thick vegetation over low hills under weird light effects is accused of being a territory of indecision: "there was that in the condition of the heath itself which resembled protracted and halting dubiousness" (chapter 2).

Uncertainty and vacillation prepare the way for unhappiness, misunderstanding, bitterness. Eustacia knows of Wildeve's attachment to Thomasin, Thomasin of his interest in Eustacia. Wildeve learns of Eustacia's interest in Clym, Clym of Eustacia's interest in Wildeve, Eustacia imagines Clym's possible interest in Thomasin and hers in him. Each is unsure of the other's affections and hence even more unwilling to commit to his or her own. One can see at once the opportunities for farce, and much of the novel, particularly the events surrounding Clym's mother's death, resembles farce, but with devastating consequences. "If you look beneath the surface of any farce you see a tragedy," Hardy tells us "and...if you blind yourself to the deeper issues of a tragedy you see a farce" (T & F, 221).

The root cause of this inability to make decisions and stick to them is fear. Just as it is a territory of "dubiousness" the heath can also "intensify the opacity of a moonless midnight to a cause of shaking and dread" (*Native*, 1.1); it is a place of fear. All the characters in the book, and indeed in all Hardy's books, can be placed along a line that goes from utterly pusillanimous (the peasant, Christian Cantle), to utterly rash (Eustacia—though that does not means she too is not also fearful). At the midpoint stands the improbable Diggory Venn, who is apprehensive, rather than fearful, cautious and resourceful, but never rash. This was the position Gabriel occupied rather more substantially in *Far from the Madding Crowd*; the person in the median position who gets it right.

What exactly are people afraid of? They are concerned that they can't trust each other. They are concerned that they can't trust themselves. Again and again they marvel at their own inability to stick to a firm course. Indeed it is part of Hardy's novelty and achievement that he appreciates modern man's struggle to assert an identity, his anxiety in the face of his own indecision, his sense that the need to become someone is perhaps too great a burden to bear. But beyond all this they are afraid of the human condition itself, of what will become of them...

> [Clym] had reached the stage in a young man's life when the grimness of the general human situation first becomes clear; and the realization of this causes ambition to halt awhile. In France it is not uncustomary to commit suicide at this stage; in England we do much better, or much worse, as the case may be. (*Native*, 3.3)

Hardy had worried again and again in his diaries that people wanted novels of manners, but he wasn't interested in manners, he was interested in emotion, the world of feeling, man's existential state. It is this underlying anxiety about the future that pushes his characters towards marriage alliances and job decisions. At the same time, when things are painful and uncertain, it can prompt a desire to be spared experience and its tough decisions altogether. Hence in *The Return of the Native*, while the novel's immediate narrative dramatizes the exciting struggle toward love and self realization, at a deeper level the atmosphere of intense trepidation that surrounds the drama is such that both characters and reader begin to wish that everything would go wrong sooner rather than later, to get it over with and have done.

It is here that the landscape plays a crucial role. If becoming someone, detaching one's individual self from the primeval heath is so painful, one could always rejoice in becoming no one again, in sinking back into the heath. When Clym ruins his eyesight studying to become a schoolmaster, he finds it surprisingly pleasurable to do the only job he is now fit for in his half-blind state: furze-cutting; it's a task that requires he wear a protective suit and mask:

> This man from Paris was now so disguised by his leather accoutrements, and by the goggles he was obliged to wear over his eyes, that his closest friend might have passed by without recognizing him. He was a brown spot in the midst of an expanse of olive-green gorse, and nothing more. Though frequently depressed in spirit when not actually at work, owing to thoughts of Eustacia's position and his mother's estrangement, when in the full swing of labour he was cheerfully disposed and calm.
>
> His daily life was of a curious microscopic sort, his whole world being limited to a circuit of a few feet from his person. His familiars were creeping and winged things, and they seemed to enroll him in their band. Bees hummed around his ears with an intimate air, and tugged at the heath and furze-flowers at his side in such numbers as to weigh them down to the sod. The strange amber-coloured butterflies which Egdon produced, and which were never seen elsewhere, quivered in the breath of his lips, alighted upon his bowed back, and sported with the glittering point of his hook as he flourished it up and down. Tribes of emerald-green grasshoppers leaped over his feet, falling awkwardly on their backs, heads, or hips, like unskilful acrobats, as chance might rule; or engaged themselves in noisy flirtations under the fern-fronds with silent ones of homely hue. Huge flies, ignorant of larders

and wire-netting, and quite in a savage state, buzzed about him without knowing that he was a man. In and out of the fern-dells snakes glided in their most brilliant blue and yellow guise, it being the season immediately following the shedding of their old skins, when their colours are brightest. Litters of young rabbits came out from their forms to sun themselves upon hillocks, the hot beams blazing through the delicate tissue of each thin-fleshed ear, and firing it to a blood-red transparency in which the veins could be seen. None of them feared him. The monotony of his occupation soothed him, and was in itself a pleasure. A forced limitation of effort offered a justification of homely courses to an unambitious man, whose conscience would hardly have allowed him to remain in such obscurity while his powers were unimpeded. (*Native*, 4.2)

In the sheer extravagance of this passage one can see how the dynamic created by problems relating to fear and courage is influencing Hardy's prose as he seeks, in the richness of language and landscape, a pleasure and refuge analogous to the comfort that "this man from Paris" finds in submitting his body to an immersion in nature that is almost an anticipation of decomposition. Freedom here, it seems, lies in surrender of identity to the present moment and untamed nature, not in the struggle for realization through career or love.

And yet one falls in love. "I love you to oppressiveness," Clym tells Eustacia before they marry. "Nothing can ensure the continuance of love," she replies. "It will evaporate like a spirit, and so I feel full of fears." She elaborates: "it will I fear end in this way: your mother will find out that you meet me, and she will influence you against me!" "The unknown," she says "always fills my mind with terrible possibilities." And again: "How terrible it would be if a time should come when I could not love you, my Clym!" And he: "Please don't say such reckless things. When we see such a time at hand we will say, 'I have outlived my faith and purpose and die'" (*Native*, 3.4).

In short, these two have already mapped out their catastrophe before it occurs. "I have feared my bliss. It has been too intense and consuming," says Eustacia (3.4). Well warned, the reader foolishly hopes disaster can be averted, as in *Far from the Madding Crowd*. And instead, everything that can go wrong does. To the point that death, when it comes, may not be such a disaster. Of Wildeve and Eustacia's corpses, laid out for burial in the final pages, we hear:

> Misfortune had struck them gracefully, cutting off their erratic histories with a catastrophic dash, instead of, as with many, attenuating each life to an uninteresting meagreness, through long years of wrinkles, neglect, and decay. (*Native*, 6.1)

Was Hardy thinking of himself as one of those condemned to an "uninteresting meagreness"? Is this what he meant earlier when he suggested that suicide was perhaps a better response to an understanding of the human condition than battling on? Certainly, the change in mood between this novel and the *Madding Crowd* of four years earlier is extraordinary, devastating. What had happened in between?

Having tied the nuptial knot in 1874 Hardy began to move his wife back and forth from the suburbs of London, a short distance from where his career was developing, to the country round Dorchester, a short distance from his family and his mother. There would be seven moves in eight years. The family the couple wanted for themselves did not arrive. Allowed to help with his writing during betrothal, indeed an integral part of his courageous bid for independence, Emma was now frozen out of her husband's work. She did not mix well in London, where she preferred to live, or at all in Dorchester, which he preferred. The class difference between them and the disapproval of their families made it hard to establish a circle of friends. Bold enough riding her horse on a Cornish beach, the childless Emma now seemed to have no role in life. Hardy, who invariably believed that every decision he had made was a rash and wrong decision, seems quite soon to have been thinking of marriage as a trap. He was seeking to establish some independence from her. Certainly, it is remarkable in *The Return of the Native* how neither of the couples who marry seem to gain any pleasure from their relationship. Before marriage yes, after it no. Having seen how happy Emma was to see the many suggestions of a parallel between herself and Bathsheba in *Far from the Madding Crowd*, Hardy must have been aware that this novel would send her the sort of message that could only make things between them worse.

More generally, it was now evident that Hardy shared the mindset that leads his characters to misery. Fearing the critics (he had wanted to die after receiving a bad review of *Desperate Remedies*), he was nevertheless writing precisely the kind of novel that would provoke them. And while good reviews were quickly forgotten, negative ones created a terrible sense of vulnerability. "Woke before it was light," he confided in his diary shortly after a negative review of *The Return of the Native*. "Felt that I had not enough staying power to hold my own in the world" (Tomalin, 170). Yet over the next ten years Hardy was to write two of the most "courageous," or courageously grim novels of the century. He was both fearful *and* courageous, indeed the two emotions seem to reinforce each other.

Published in 1891, *Tess of the D'Urbervilles* immediately warns us that our experience of reading the book will be one of waiting for catastrophe. No sooner are Tess and her siblings introduced than we hear:

> All these young souls were passengers in the Durbeyfield ship, entirely dependent on the judgement of the two Durbeyfield adults for their pleasures, their necessities, their health, even their existence. If the heads of the Durbeyfield household chose to sail into difficulty, disaster, starvation, disease, degradation, death, thither were these half-dozen little captives under hatches compelled to sail with them—six helpless creatures, who had never been asked if they wished for life on any terms, much less if they wished for it on such hard conditions. (*Tess*, chapter 3)

Disaster is not long in coming. Roused at night to drive her drunken father's beehives to market, Tess falls asleep at the reins of the cart and the family's horse is killed, a ruinous loss. As the animal is buried Tess "regarded herself in the light of a murderess" (chapter 4); that is, she internalizes as moral failing and guilt what the reader understands to be a consequence of parental carelessness and bad luck. This she will continue to do for the whole duration of the book.

Since her family is now in economic trouble Tess is sent into service with a family who may or may not be distant aristocratic relatives. Improvident as ever, her mother dresses her in such a way that "might cause her to be estimated as a woman when she was not much more than a child" (chapter 7).

Though "naturally...courageous," after her accident with the cart Tess becomes "exceedingly timid" about wheeled transport, something the rakish Alec d'Urberville spots at once when he picks her up in his dog cart to bring her to her new home. First he accelerates wildly, terrifying her, then demands a kiss as the price of slowing down. It's a replay of Troy and Bathsheba. Beside herself with fear, Tess accepts, then changes her mind when he slows, at which he accuses her of breaking her word. Since this is something she knows she must not do (ethical polarity), she now accepts the kiss, protesting, "But I thought you would be kind to me, and protect me" (chapter 8).

With this ironic back and forth between fear/courage and propriety/impropriety Hardy opens the way to Tess's downfall. Disaster strikes after an evening of merriment with other servants. Walking home in the dark, an argument develops between Tess and another, rather aggressive, perhaps drunken girl. Fearful, Tess sensibly declines to fight, then is fatally rash when Alec appears on his horse and offers to carry her home. Hardy remarks that "coming as [Alec's] invitation did at the particular juncture when fear and indignation at these adversaries could be transformed by a spring of the foot into a triumph over them, she abandoned herself to her impulse" (chapter 10). That is, she climbs up on Alec's horse. Again, a natural impulse to do with winning and losing, or even declaring herself more upper class than lower, provokes a transgression on the moral plane, though Tess has not at this point remotely thought of events in moral terms. Such an "explanation" has the effect of persuading us that the question we must ask of our heroine is not, in what way did she sin, but rather, how was it that she made such a bad mistake?

At some point on the ride home, Alec has sex with her. Does he rape her? Does she simply give way? Again, the actual moment of erotic contact is elided. We don't know. Again we are given the sense of something fatal having happened without our or Tess's properly noticing. "An immeasurable social chasm was to divide our heroine's personality thereafter from that previous self of hers..." (chapter 11).

Pregnant, Tess refuses help from Alec, returns home, gives birth, loses the child to illness, and is generally shamed and disgraced. To escape this stigma, she again leaves home and travels to a distant farm to work as a milkmaid, and here she falls in love with Angel Clare.

Why, after their romantic disappointments, do Hardy's characters always come back for more? And why, after having already been criticized for writing about sex and having made it clear how much the criticisms hurt, was Hardy returning to the subject? It was irresistible, it was life itself, and the impulse to go courageously toward it, declaring one's independence (because to be independent was to be properly alive) vied constantly with the impulse to self preservation. Tess embodies that irresistibility. On the other hand, contemplation of Tess's beauty always creates an atmosphere of intense trepidation. Here is Tess in the milking parlour when Angel enters unseen.

> She was yawning, and he saw the red interior of her mouth as if it had been a snake's. She had stretched one arm so high above her coiled-up cable of hair that he could see its satin delicacy above the sunburn; her face was flushed with sleep, and her eyelids hung heavy over their pupils. The brimfulness of her nature breathed from her. It was a moment when a woman's soul is more incarnate than at any other time; when the most spiritual beauty bespeaks itself flesh, and sex takes the outside place in the presentation.
>
> Then those eyes flashed brightly through their filmy heaviness, before the remainder of her face was well awake. With an oddly compounded look of gladness, shyness and surprise, she exclaimed—
>
> "O Mr Clare! How you frightened me." (chapter 27)

Hardy had said that he wished "to demolish the doll of English fiction,"[9] but to suppose that he sought to do this as part of a campaign for female emancipation would be to misunderstand ("my husband's interest in the Suffrage cause is nil," remarked his wife, "in spite of Tess"[10]). What mattered for Hardy was the freedom to evoke the lure and terror of sexual experience. The more seductive the descriptions of Tess, the greater the danger. Her opening mouth is a snake's. Without this sense of two "tremulous lives" moving towards "terrifying bliss" (chapter 29) the couple's eventual failure to consummate their love would be inexplicable. Hardy's genius is to have us experience the oneness of fear and desire and courage in the mind set he moves in. Life is unspeakably desirable, I cannot not try to grasp it. And it is simultaneously terrifying: even as I seek to grasp it, I will look for reasons for not doing so. Reading about Tess is a huge pleasure, but frightening and painful. I pick the book up, then put it down again. I read on, then almost wish I hadn't.

After the two agree to marry, Tess wrestles with the question of whether to tell Angel about her experience with Alec before the wedding. She writes a letter which he doesn't see, because it slips under a doormat. The secret still untold, the couple get married. At last they are alone. No one can interfere. The sexual experience towards which a hundred and more very lush pages have been leading is imminent. Clare, however, chooses this of all moments to confess to a sin, some years before, of "eight and forty hours dissipation with a stranger" (chapter 34). Tess instantly forgives him and responds with her own sad history. Angel instantly rejects her. There will be no love-making.

The scene is an extraordinary one. Suddenly both lovers' fears are entirely confirmed. For Angel, Tess is a different person, the decision to marry a girl from the lower classes has proved a terrible error: "I repeat, the woman I have been loving is not you." With "terror upon her white face," Tess feels all the weight of Victorian morals and class division come down upon her. Meantime the reader cannot help but feel that both partners were all too ready to see "the terrifying bliss" of sexual love thwarted. Sooner than expected, "Having nothing more to fear," Tess falls asleep. Two days later, of her own accord, she returns home (chapter 35).

After one disaster from undesired consummation and another from failure to achieve consummation intensely desired, Tess's story gets worse. Angel flees to Brazil. Alec invites her to return to him; she resists but following her father's death her family is plunged into poverty. Alec will help out only if she becomes his concubine. She does. Too late Angel returns, full of remorse. Meeting him only heightens Tess's sense of what she has lost. Provoked by Alec, she loses her head and, in a wild rash moment, kills him. Despite Angel's feeble attempts to keep her away from the police, she quickly lapses into a sense that all is lost, and that it would be better if she were executed sooner rather than later. There have already been a number of occasions when she has looked forward to being "grassed down and forgotten" (chapter 14).

Tess was the first of Hardy's novels to provoke intense criticism and controversy. Since he had been obliged to cut all explicit sexual references from the serialized edition but had later reinstated them for the volume edition, he must have expected that some readers would be scandalized. Can we assume, then, that Hardy's literary success to date had given him the courage now to say what he thought, refusing the kind of compromise that was made at the end of *Return of the Native*; or perhaps that, paradoxically, the more successful he was the gloomier his vision became?

By the end of the 1870s Hardy had decided that he really wanted to live in Dorset, near his family, his mother, in rural seclusion. Emma, however, like Eustacia, wanted to live in town. But when in city society, her boldness, the quality Hardy had initially admired in her, often came across as mere caprice and rash empty-headedness. He became anxious whenever she opened her mouth in company. On the other hand when they were in the country she had nothing to do. She wanted to be part of his writing life, for his career to be a joint project, whereas he needed to be independent and free.

In 1880, living in London at this point, the problem was partly redressed by Hardy's falling ill with a bladder complaint. It was a painful condition that would recur throughout his life. Doctors talked about internal haemorrhage but without having any instruments to confirm this diagnosis. Since the condition was eventually cured, or alleviated by a six-month stay in bed, we are evidently not talking about acute infection. Most likely it was something now referred to as pelvic pain syndrome, or chronic prostatitis, a condition that, judging by reports of symptoms, has afflicted any number of writers (Coleridge, Dostoevsky, Beckett, and indeed the present author). The combination of bowed and seated posture and constant mental tension appear to be contributing factors. But however serious the pain, Hardy never stopped writing through the period, since he was under contract for a serialized novel, *The Laodiceans*, and would never risk the wrath of his publishers. Again this suggests that there was no fever and nothing that undermined his mental strength. Meantime, with her husband laid up and needing her help to copy manuscripts and contact publishers, Emma regained some power in the relationship. The upshot would be that at the end of the six months she agreed to the purchase of a plot of land in Dorset to build a house there.

Systemic psychologists refer to those values constructed around fear and courage as the semantic of freedom. Fear limits freedom. The agoraphobic is too frightened to go outside, the claustrophobic too scared to get in a lift, or a car or an aeroplane. All his life Hardy had oscillated between gestures of extreme independence and extreme cautiousness. He was always ready to return home, or to the protection of his wife, but equally ready to strike out for London. He was ready to write novels that were terrifying and offensive to the Victorians, then to fall back on the most innocuous little comedies. Again and again, he writes letters proposing bold solutions to publishers, but only if they will not give offence. In general, he is obsessed by the dangers of giving offence, then gives it anyway, then feels he has been rash and steps back. If his initial strategy as a writer had been to build up a body of commercially successful work that would grant him freedom later, he now found himself locked in a frustrating marriage and imprisoned in serialization contracts that obliged him to work constantly, sometimes frenetically, even when reduced to bed. From now on he would seek to be more free at least in his writing.

Shortly after his recovery, he built his house in Dorset. Designed by Hardy himself, Max Gate, as it was called, was small, unimaginative, and surrounded by a protective belt of trees that he would never allow anyone to prune. Guests complained it was gloomy and suffocating. Was this freedom or a prison? While the house was being built Hardy wrote *Two on a Tower*, about an unhappily married lady who falls in love with a younger, lower-class intellectual. Once settled in the house, he started the more disquieting *Mayor of Casterbridge*, in which a drunken young man makes the fatal (surreal) "mistake" of selling his wife at a fair. She returns to haunt him eighteen years later just as he is ready to set up with a young woman he loves.

Meantime Hardy's own marriage had sunk back into its previous torpor. In a later letter Emma noted that "at fifty a man's feelings too often take a new course altogether. Eastern ideas of matrimony secretly pervade his thoughts, and he wearies of the most perfect, and suitable wife chosen in his earlier life" (Tomalin, 273). In 1889 she decided they must henceforth sleep in separate beds. She had begun a diary and was writing furious things about him. Hardy was writing flirtatious letters to lady fans. He would meet them in London, ingratiate himself by pushing their stories on his publishers, write love letters and quaint poems to them. But never, so far as we know, did he go to bed with them. Here is one such poem:

She wore a new "terra-cotta" dress,
And we stayed, because of the pelting storm,
Within the hansom's dry recess,
Though the horse had stopped; yea, motionless
    We sat on, snug and warm.

Then the downpour ceased, to my sharp sad pain,
And the glass that had screened our forms before
Flew up, and out she sprang to her door:
I should have kissed her if the rain
    Had lasted a minute more.
             (*Hardy Poems*, 312)

This was the state of play when *Tess* was written: a timid man was on the brink of adultery, protesting he would have got there if only the rain hadn't stopped. Critics constantly ask where Hardy's pessimism comes from. What had he been reading? Is it Schopenhauer or Ecclesiastes? Perhaps it would be more useful to ask, where was the pessimism *taking him*, what would be the effect of such grim stories on the dynamic of his life? Pessimism is perhaps more comprehensible as a tool than a credo. Someone who has managed to convince himself that the world is simultaneously as enticing and as forbidding and unhappy as it appears in *Tess*, that the slightest move towards unspeakable pleasure will bring the community down on you in the most terrifying way, is not likely, or *less* likely to become an adulterer.

But if this was the message Hardy was sending to himself—the pleasure, then the rap on the hands—what was the effect on the world around him? His wife disliked the book. She could hardly have done otherwise. Its longings and rancour could only be disturbing to her. And while some critics were enthralled, others were appalled, especially with the reinstated sexual content when the novel appeared in volume form. "It is a queer story and seems to have been published in a queer manner," complained Mowbray Morris.[11] What he resented most was Hardy's causing the reader to hope, then piling on the pain and at the same time insisting that Tess remained pure. He and other critics repeatedly attacked the subtitle; far from being a "pure woman," Tess was a "little harlot." The desire to get back to a reassuringly moral reading of the story along a polarity good/evil is evident. Tess ends badly because she behaves badly and Hardy is behaving badly by not acknowledging that. "Has the common feeling of humanity against seduction, adultery and murder no basis in the heart of things?" protests Mowbray Morris. And he insists, "It is the very foundation of human society" (Cox, 233).

Morris was right; core values were under attack. For his part, Hardy registered only these negative criticisms, not the book's many positive reviews, as if such aggressive censure offered him *exactly* the confirmation he was looking for that the world was indeed the very dangerous place he had described in *Tess*: it was mad, he concluded, to expose oneself in fiction just "to be shot at" (T & F, 254). At no point did a positive review encourage him to believe that life might be lived differently, an affair enjoyed, a divorce obtained. Other Victorians were doing this and surviving, Wilkie Collins and George Eliot to name but two. Dickens had quite brutally separated from the wife and mother of his ten children decades before. But for Hardy this was simply, as Ugazio would put it, "a forbidden story." He could neither write about nor experience himself the kind of unpunished freedom he appeared to yearn for.

But having said he wouldn't expose himself to be shot at, Hardy proceeded to do just that. For if *Tess of the D'Urbervilles* was courageous, four years later *Jude the Obscure* was near suicidal. "Jude the obscene," one critic wrote, "a shameful nightmare" (Tomalin, 259).

Renouncing the reassuring descriptions of country life, the pleasing chorus of village rustics, with *Jude* Hardy pushes his negative vision to the limit. A poor orphan trying to hide from life in scholarship has a rude awakening when seduced by a raw country girl. Married and separated in a matter of pages, he falls in love with his refined cousin, Sue, a girl so terrified by sex that when she marries a much older man to escape Jude she denies him consummation, then later returns to Jude in the hope that he will be willing to live with her without sex (because married to someone else), then gives herself to him sexually only when she fears that physical need will drive him back to his wife.

Coincidences and misfortunes abound. When the child got from Jude's wife kills the children got from Sue and then hangs himself, it is the death of hope *tout court*, the proof that all attempts to achieve happiness will end in disaster; it would have been better never to have tried. To provoke his Victorian readers further, Hardy again, as in

Tess, offers an ending mockingly in line with their moral convictions: appalled by the death of her children, Sue gets religion and returns to her husband while Jude is seduced by his wife and goes back to her shortly before his death. "What has Providence done to Mr Hardy," wrote the author's friend Edmund Gosse, reviewing the book, "that he should rise up in the arable land of Wessex and shake his fist at his Creator?" (Tomalin, 222)

This was surely the break point. Hardy had written openly of sexual problems that people close to him knew were to do with his own marriage and frustrations. He had spoken explicitly of marriage as a trap. "Why can't we agree to free each other?" begs Sue of her husband. Yet at the same time he was suggesting that the community's principles were so internalized in his protagonists' minds that there was no question of escaping them. "We must conform!..." says Sue at the bitter climax of the novel. "I am cowed into submission. I have no more fighting strength left; no more enterprise. I am beaten, beaten!" (*Jude*, 6.3) Victorian principles prevail, albeit as a decaying albatross round the necks of these would-be revolutionaries. And Hardy stayed in his gloomy Dorset home, adding an outside staircase so he could move between study and garden without meeting Emma.

What broke in the end was not this way of life, but Hardy's will to go on writing novels. If one function of his narrative pessimism had been to keep him in his marriage, despite his unhappiness, this "advantage" was now outweighed by the deeper bitterness the novel itself created in the marriage—his wife openly announcing her disgust with the book to dinner guests—and again the extreme hostility of a wide area of the press. Hardy, like Sue and Jude, was now cowed into submission, lost any will to go on struggling with his dilemma. Quite probably he accepted the situation with the same relief that Tess accepts her death, especially since the scandal of the book turned it into a considerable commercial success that now made him as independent financially as he was trapped domestically. From now on he would only write poetry, where, he claimed, the same strong opinions could be expressed without the negative response, largely because the absence of narrative and the attractions of lyricism prevented the same ferocious engagement on the part of the reader. A disembodied idea is much less dangerous than an embodied one. In a letter in 1888 he remarked: "if there is any way of getting a melancholy satisfaction out of life it lies in dying, so to speak, before one is out of the flesh; by which I mean putting on the manners of ghosts, wandering in their haunts, and taking their view of surrounding things. To think of life as passing away is a sadness, to think of it as past is at least tolerable. Hence even when I enter into a room to pay a simple morning call, I have unconsciously the habit of regarding the scene as if I were a spectre not solid enough to influence my environment" (Tomalin, 224). The relation of such a wish to the fear/courage polarity is evident, as equally there is a parallel between the desire to be beyond engagement and responsibility and Tess's desire to forget her body in contemplation of the stars, or again Clym's happiness submerging himself in vegetation and insect life. Hardy yearns for a place beyond fear, desire, and the need to muster courage. He gave up novel-writing, one might hazard, to look for that place and that ghostly persona in poetry.

Here is *Afterwards*:

When the Present has latched its postern behind my tremulous stay,
    And the May month flaps its glad green leaves like wings,
Delicate-filmed as new-spun silk, will the neighbours say,
    "He was a man who used to notice such things"?

If it be in the dusk when, like an eyelid's soundless blink,
    The dewfall-hawk comes crossing the shades to alight
Upon the wind-warped upland thorn, a gazer may think,
    "To him this must have been a familiar sight."

If I pass during some nocturnal blackness, mothy and warm,
    When the hedgehog travels furtively over the lawn,
One may say, "He strove that such innocent creatures should
        come to no harm,
    But he could do little for them; and now he is gone."

If, when hearing that I have been stilled at last, they stand at the door,
    Watching the full-starred heavens that winter sees,
Will this thought rise on those who will meet my face no more,
    "He was one who had an eye for such mysteries"?

And will any say when my bell of quittance is heard in the gloom,
    And a crossing breeze cuts a pause in its outrollings,
Till they rise again, as they were a new bell's boom,
    "He hears it not now, but used to notice such things"?

                                                    (*Hardy Poems*, 553)

All Hardy's old anxieties are here, but so quietly and beautifully expressed we hardly notice. The poet's has been a "tremulous" life, death is already behind him, aestheticized in the tolling bell; his concern about his reputation is presented modestly as he wonders whether people will remember how he observed the natural world that the poem then immerses itself in. A rapacious bird of prey becomes the charming "dewfall-hawk"; the fact that this bird could be responsible for the death of the "furtive hedgehog" of the next stanza is discreetly left unmentioned. Hardy "strove that such innocent creatures should come to no harm. But he could do little for them; and now he is gone"—so much for the possibility of positive action in the world. In the fourth stanza the starry heavens remain the "mystery" they always were. There is no God. Finally the bell of "quittance" suggests "discharge from a debt or obligation."[12] Hardy is relieved to be gone. All life's passions have been elided, not just the fatal consummation, Bathsheba's first kiss with Troy, Tess's sex with Alec, but the whole damn narrative. The pessimism is so elegantly put that no one could possibly object. Above all there are no women.

D. H. Lawrence accepted a commission to write a study of Thomas Hardy in 1914. Having signed the contract, he typically asserted his independence by using the book to develop his own views, leaving Hardy out of the picture for many pages at a time. Essentially Lawrence's position is this, that "The final aim of every living thing, creature or being is the full achievement of itself";[13] however, people nevertheless assume that "life is the great struggle for self preservation" (p. 13), this out of "a cowardice that will not let us be" (p. 17). Hardy, he says, depicts exceptional characters struggling towards full achievement, but then contrives to have them destroyed, indeed "cowed" (p. 30) by the spirit of self preservation in the community. So, in obedience to the notion that "the spirit of Love must always succumb before the blind, stupid, but overwhelming power of the Law," Hardy goes "against himself" to "stand with the average against the exception" (p. 43), and all this "in order to explain his own sense of failure" (p. 92).

Lawrence does not tell us what Hardy's "failure" might be, but it is clear that, having understood how the scales are tipped towards fear in Hardy's work, Lawrence is defining himself in contrast. It is as if Hardy were the kind of novelist he thinks he might have been had he not faced and overcome his fears. His poetic will be declaredly the opposite of Hardy's. Instead of using the novel to keep novelist and reader anchored in conformity, perhaps with some vague reference to future times when people may be freer, he will use it as a tool to open up a world of possibility and liberty, *now* and against all opposition.

The reasons why Lawrence saw an affinity between himself and the older writer are clear enough. Born in 1885, Lawrence, like Hardy, was a sickly child in a family where security depended on manual labour for which he was judged unfit.[14] His mother, like Hardy's, was at once protective, instilling a sense of life's danger, yet ambitious for him, ready to push him out early into the world, a situation bound to generate anxiety. Unlike Hardy, however, Lawrence was not the eldest child, but the fourth of five, and would have to wait until an older second son died to become mother's favourite. He grew up in a situation of competition. His mother then died when he was 25 and with the subsequent break-up of the family there was no home to return to. That was exactly the age at which Hardy had run back to his mother from London.

The most striking difference, however, between the two families was the level of parental conflict in the Lawrence household, of which the declaredly autobiographical *Sons and Lovers* gives a vivid account. Paul Morel is Lawrence's alter ego; very soon we hear how his schoolteacher mother uses moral censure as a weapon against the physically stronger miner father; the polarity of winning and losing in this family is always more important than that of right and wrong.

> There began a battle between the husband and wife, a fearful bloody battle that ended only with the death of one. She fought to make him undertake his own responsibilities, to make him fulfil his obligations. But he was too different from her. His nature was purely sensuous, and she strove to make him moral, religious. (*Sons*, chapter 1)

Similarly, towards the end of the book, Paul's girlfriend Miriam, resisting his sexual advances, reflects that he "was arguing God onto his own side, because he wanted his own way, and his own pleasure. There was a long battle between him and her" (chapter 9).

The language of conflict is so pervasive throughout *Sons and Lovers* that one might suppose that it establishes the dominant polarity, that what matters above all is to find a position in the winner/loser polarity. Not only are there chapter headings such as "The Birth of Paul, and another Battle," "Strife in Love," and "The Defeat of Miriam," but every incident and every relationship is described in terms of conflict and competition. The Morel children are most loved when they win prizes in competition with others. Mrs Morel "bullies" the clergyman over his sermons (chapter 2), fights with "her enemy, the pot man" (chapter 4), the eldest son William fights with the neighbours' children, fights his mother over his girlfriends (whom he considers as so many conquests) and later his fiancée, Louisa Western. Paul will fight with Miriam, his mother, his married mistress Clara, and, brutally and physically, with her husband, Baxter Dawes. Watching the shadows a fire casts on the walls, it seems to the infant Paul that his room is "full of men who battled silently" (chapter 4).

However, if conflict is to the fore in a way it never is in Hardy, attitudes toward conflict are governed by fear, each character being quickly placed by the way in which fear or caution, courage or rashness, predisposes them to conflict. Morel is a "heedless man, careless of danger" (chapter 5); he has "not a grain of physical fear" (chapter 1) but is "afraid to seem too jubilant" in his wife's presence (chapter 1) and "always ran away from the battle with himself" (chapter 1). Physically weaker, Mrs Morel is impelled to fight out of fear of being left without financial support—"My only fear was that he'd pawn something" (chapter 2), she says when her husband runs away. Miriam fears any engagement that could be painful; she is even afraid of offering corn to a hen for fear of having her fingers pecked.

The most subtle nuancing of the relation between fear and conflict comes in the presentation of Paul. He is afraid of the battle between his parents: "the children lay silent in suspense, waiting for a lull in the wind to hear what their father was doing. He might hit their mother again. There was a feeling of horror, a kind of bristling in the darkness and a sense of blood" (chapter 4). As a result of such experiences the boy recoils from every form of engagement with the adult world. Sent to get his father's wages, he is too terrified to speak in front of the miners. This is the first occasion on which fear is put in relation to self consciousness: "Paul was suffering convulsions of self consciousness" (chapter 4).

However, to withdraw from the fray is to risk exclusion from life. When Paul and Arthur cannot find friends to play and fight with, they look "anxiously" about and feel "genuine desolation" (chapter 4). To find their companions is a pleasure, even though "The six would fight, hate with a fury of hatred, and flee home in terror" (chapter 4).

Paul begins to see the need to overcome fear in order to engage in life's struggle when his mother takes him for a job interview at a factory making artificial limbs, Jordan's. Paul, like Hardy's Jude, has no desire to grow up. His ambition is for a quiet life beside his mother. On the other hand, the family spirit of competition has given him the habit of "measuring people against himself" (chapter 5). The verb "shrink" becomes important here to establish a connection between fear and problems of engagement. Both Paul and his mother "shrank" from life (chapter 5), but she had nevertheless learned to fight for her rights.

The interview is presented, hilariously, as a battle in which Paul is too fearfully self conscious to assert himself until Mr Jordan corrects his translation of "doigts" as "fingers," explaining that the word means "toes," at which Paul becomes "defiant"—" 'Well, it does mean fingers,' the boy persisted" (chapter 5). Fighting back from timidity, he is given the job.

So much of the critical comment on *Sons and Lovers* concentrates on Paul's morbid attachment to his mother and sexual difficulties with Miriam but it seems useful to remember that from the beginning he is fearful of engaging in life at any level. Lawrence's complaint that his sexuality was blocked by mother love can thus be seen as partly an alibi for, or at least integrated with, a generally fearful disposition. The similarity with Hardy is evident.

Once engaged in life's conflict, fears multiply and the most curious fear of all, the one that determines that the dominant polarity will be fear/courage rather than winning/losing, is the fear of victory. In situations of crisis, fear arouses hatred and one is tempted to crush one's antagonist. But to do so can have disastrous consequences. After the apparent victory involved in locking his wife out of the house, Morel experiences a "shrinking, a diminishing in his assurance" (chapter 2). Eventually, Mrs Morel, weaker physically but stronger psychologically, draws all the children into an alliance against Morel, who is now "shut out from all family affairs" (chapter 4). But the completeness of her victory is her ruin; she is "hurt" (chapter 5) by her inability to love her husband and forced to turn for fulfilment to unsatisfactory relationships with her children.

Since it seems legitimate to identify Lawrence's concerns with Paul's in this avowedly autobiographical novel, we can say that the author is confronting two problems: how to overcome fear as a prerequisite of self realization and how to behave in such a way that once engaged in life one neither destroys nor is destroyed. Love is insistently presented as a battle to possess or be possessed, yet for either party to get complete control is disastrous for both. In the later essay, "Morality and the Novel," Lawrence remarks that to strike the right balance in such relationships requires "courage above all things."[15]

Like *Tess*, *Sons and Lovers* has at its core a frustratingly long courtship. In *Tess* consummation is denied when, hearing of Tess's past, Angel declares that "You were one person; now you are another" (*Tess*, chapter 35). As Tess acquires a history and an individuality—her relationship with Alec, her dead child—she ceases to be an idealized object of desire and Angel is unable to love her. In *Sons and Lovers*, in a reverse process, Paul finds that to make love to Miriam he has to stop seeing her as an individual and discover the impersonal in both her and himself. We hear that "he shrank from the physical contact" because Miriam always called him back from "a swoon of passion" to "the littleness, the personal relationship" (chapter 11). Given Miriam's vocation for spirituality this is also a disembodied relationship. "I am quite ghostish, disembodied," Paul protests (chapter 8). Here we might recall Hardy's pleasure at the thought that a ghostly self would not be "solid enough to influence [his] environment" (Tomalin, 224). Tess too in one of her moods of resignation talks of her pleasure in contemplating the stars and feeling she is "hundreds and hundreds o'miles away from [her] body" (*Tess*, chapter 18). In his determination to live, however, Paul cannot see his feelings of disembodiment positively and speaks instead of shedding the self-conscious individuality that he has now identified as the source of fear and inhibition: "She lost all her self-control, was exposed in fear. And he knew, before he could kiss her, he must drive something out of himself" (chapter 8).

After finally making love Paul enjoys an experience of being "smeared away into the beyond," "melt[ing] out into darkness"; it is a "reaching-out to death" (chapter 11), in short a loss of selfhood comparable to the experiences of Tess and Clym when they work in the fields. But while in Hardy such experiences are consolatory, following defeat, in Lawrence they are enabling, and come as a consequence of consummation. A discovery of the "impersonal fire of desire" makes engagement with the world possible (chapter 11). Later, his whole sexual relationship with Clara is shown to have been "impersonal" (chapter 23).

Having understood the liberating consequences of shedding conscious selfhood and its fears, Lawrence carries out a transformation that would become one of the hallmarks of his mature work. Previously, Paul had persuaded himself he must not make love to Miriam for fear of damaging someone who is "good," ethical considerations bolstering his fear: "Something in me shrinks from her like hell—she's so good, when I'm not good" (chapter 10). Now he decides that fear itself is morally wrong: "Don't you think," he asks Miriam, "we have been too fierce in what they call purity? Don't you think that to be so much afraid and averse is a sort of dirtiness?" And again, "Some sort of perversity in our souls...makes us not want, get away from, the very thing we want. We have to fight against that" (chapter 10).

At this point, it is not, as Victorian society saw it, the (premarital) sex that is immoral but the lovers' fear of it and Lawrence can henceforward transform the struggle to overcome fear into a moral crusade. Hence certain developments in his later work, his exploration of different levels of consciousness, his constant comparison between modern and "primitive" psyches, his habit of fashioning a personal morality complete with a religious aura in contrast to conventional morality, can all be seen as the fruit of his need to confront fear and push beyond it. While Hardy's narratives, we might say, confirm that it is appropriate to be fearful, even if pride demands that I make a gesture of courage before retreating into conformity, Lawrence's dramatize the absolute necessity of fighting fear, of never succumbing to mere conformity; reading Hardy, we wait for catastrophe which will excuse renunciation, reading Lawrence we watch the developments of a struggle, and in the novels of the mature period are invited to engage in that struggle ourselves.

It is at the point that fear is identified as the enemy and attacked that Lawrence's problems with the critics begin. "To our grief and our amazement," writes one reviewer of the second half of *Sons and Lovers*, "the book suffers a sea change...We revolt in weariness from incessant scenes of sexual passion."[16] As Lawrence focuses fearlessly on sexual experience in *The Rainbow* and then *Women in Love*, he necessarily arouses the ire of the critics. James Douglas in his notorious *Star* review of *The Rainbow* claimed that "No novel in the English language [is] so utterly lacking in verbal reticence"; its characters, he complained, were "creatures...immeasurably lower than the lowest animal in the zoo" (Draper, 93).

Together with the content of the books it was understood that Lawrence's style had also changed. "The thud thud thud of the hectic phrases is intolerably wearisome," Douglas remarked, establishing a "dull monotonous tune of spiritless sensuality" (Draper, 93). In a concluding passage, extraordinary for its adoption of Lawrence's own vocabulary and vehemence, Douglas insisted that "The artist is not his own lawgiver. He must bow before the will of the generations of man" (Draper, 94). Like a Lawrence character whom fear has prompted to seek the annihilation of his opponent, Douglas went on to invoke the banning of *The Rainbow*, speaking of a moral "battle" in which, as a matter of urgent "self-preservation," "every man and woman must take sides" (Draper, 94).

Lawrence's new style thus created, outside his fiction, exactly the sort of relationship he discusses in it.[17] Middleton Murry was reacting to this development when he spoke of Lawrence as having given up "deliberately, the pretence of being an artist...His aim was to discover authority, not to create art."[18] The implication is that the reader's response to Lawrence, in what Gregory Bateson would have recognized as a schismogenetic process, must be to accept, or more likely struggle against, Lawrence's credo. Curiously, this is exactly what Lawrence seemed to want. "Whoever reads me will be in the thick of the scrimmage," he declared.[19]

Having decided that fearful self consciousness and limiting conformity were essentially constructed in language, it was inevitable that Lawrence would launch an attack on standard English and celebrate liberating mental states beyond rational thinking; hence such syntactically transgressive (and courageous) phrases as "she was destroyed into perfect consciousness,"[20] or "they were glad and could forget perfectly" (*Women*, 397). The techniques he developed and their many implications have been meticulously explored by critics excited by this experimentalism,[21] but the tendency to present Lawrence as carrying out some sort of dispassionate linguistic research is misleading. Lawrence's innovations make sense when one appreciates the underlying semantic of freedom which drives them, the determination to assume a position of independence and courage, with but one caveat—one's opponent must never be crushed. The virtue of the novel form he felt was precisely that plot and story constantly undercut any narrow didactic position taken by the author and hence it was unlikely you could ever grind an opponent into the ground. This was the sense of his famous injunction: "Never trust the artist. Trust the tale."[22]

Perhaps the closest analogy to Lawrence's desired relationship with the reader is his description of the wrestling match that Birkin and Gerald enjoy in *Women in Love*. The two fight naked until both men are so exhausted they fall into a trance, "quite unconscious," but with Birkin, Lawrence's alter ego, lying on top (*Women*, 349).

Even allowing for the half a century between them, the social and cultural changes and the impact of the Great War, it is remarkable how Hardy and Lawrence follow opposite but related trajectories according to the way they dealt with the tension between fearfulness and self assertion that their families bequeathed them. Hardy's marriage to Emma is a cautious adventure, Lawrence's a flagrant breach of convention, as he walks off with a married and foreign woman who already has three children. Hardy keeps marital strife strictly private; the Lawrences yell and hurl saucepans at each other in public. Hardy builds himself a house not far from his village home and surrounds it with dark trees; Lawrence never owns a home of his own and leaves England to measure himself against a succession of alien cultures under the hottest of suns. Hardy negotiates with censorship and trembles at criticism; Lawrence flouts the censors and thrives on upsetting the critics. Unbelieving, Hardy becomes a regular churchgoer and observes all conventional proprieties; Lawrence fashions a morality of his own which pronounces a hymn like "Lead, Kindly Light" profoundly evil (*Study*, 176). Hardy destroys most of his private letters and papers. Lawrence destroys nothing. Hardy is "seriously" ill twice, but without any known pathology or long-term consequences; on both occasions the illness leads him to renounce independence and fall back on the protective female figure in his life, mother or wife;

Lawrence is frequently at death's door but denies that he has tuberculosis and carries on regardless, complaining only that weakness prevents him from physical combat with his wife. Hardy lived to a ripe and celebrated old age; Lawrence died at 44, worn out with his fighting and travelling. Neither man suffered from feelings of guilt.

To read Hardy and then Lawrence is to shift from one position to the other inside the same semantic of courage and fear. Understandably, most negative responses to Hardy's novels dissolve as Victorian propriety gives way to contemporary mores; what remains is the need to position oneself in response to his immense pessimism; the critical strategy has generally been to pretend that such pessimism was appropriate given the moral climate in Victorian England, which is always assumed to be as bad as Hardy claimed it was, forgetting the vast sales of his books and the many prominent people who did exactly the things he might have liked to have done with relative impunity. This merely suggests the difficulty critics have in facing the notion that some literature can be profoundly negative and defeatist in spirit. Hardy's writing is immensely seductive and powerfully draws us into a particular mental atmosphere. But one simply cannot make for it the kind of claims that people like to make for literature, that it is liberating, for example, or empowering. Quite the contrary. At most it is beautifully consoling, from a position of defeatism; more frequently it stirs up feelings of angry impotence. Lawrence, on the other hand, responding aggressively to fear, continues to provoke controversy since he flagrantly takes up positions which run counter to today's political correctness and anyway does not even wish for people to agree with him, only to engage in fierce debate. So eagerly did he await negative reviews that he often had his responses to them ready even before his books were published. In the end the pleasure in reading Lawrence is not agreeing with him, but facing him, fearlessly.

The enormous achievement of both writers was to draw us into the tensions that formed their mental world. If both writers are special it is because both have given us themselves, their positions, with all their instability, anxiety, and exhilaration. That said, it is hard (for me) not to feel that Hardy, whose work I love, can be a truly toxic, imprisoning influence, while Lawrence, however infuriating, is always liberating. In this sense they push the reader to the opposite extremes of the semantic they moved in.

Notes

1. Claire Tomalin, *Thomas Hardy: The Time-Torn Man* (London: Viking, 2006), 288. Hereafter cited as "Tomalin."

2. Thomas Hardy, *Jude the Obscure* (New York: Signet Classics, 1999), 1.2. Hereafter cited as "*Jude*" with part and chapter references.

3. Thomas and Florence Hardy, *Thomas Hardy* (London: Wordsworth Editions, 2007), 48. Hereafter cited as "T & F."

4. See G. W. Sherman, *The Pessimism of Thomas Hardy* (Madison, NJ: Fairleigh Dickinson University Press, 1976), 114, and Birgit Plietzsch, *The Novels of Thomas Hardy as a Product of Nineteenth-Century Social, Economic and Cultural Change* (Berlin: Tenea, 2004), 162; also Peter Widdowson, *Hardy in History: A Study in Literary Sociology* (London: Routledge, 1989), 135.

5. Edmund Gosse, quoted in M. Ray, *Thomas Hardy Remembered* (London: Ashgate, 2007), 214. Hereafter cited as "Gosse."

6. Thomas Hardy, *Far from the Madding Crowd* (Oxford University Press, 2002), chapter 28. Hereafter cited as "*Madding Crowd*."

7. Michael Millgate, *Thomas Hardy: A Biography* (Oxford University Press, 1982), 112.

8. Thomas Hardy, *Tess of the D'Urbervilles* (London: Penguin, 2003), chapter 32. Hereafter cited as "*Tess*."

9. *The Collected Letters of Thomas Hardy*, Vol. I, ed. Richard Purdy and Michael Millgate (Oxford: Clarendon Press, 1979), 250.

10. *Letters of Emma and Florence Hardy*, ed. Michael Millgate (Oxford: Clarendon Press, 1996), 6.

11. *Thomas Hardy, the Critical Heritage*, ed. Reginald Cox (London: Routledge, 1979), 217. Hereafter cited as "Cox."

12. Merriam-Webster online dictionary.

13. D. H Lawrence, *Study of Thomas Hardy and Other Essays* (Cambridge University Press, 1985), 12. Hereafter cited as "*Study*."

14. Of Lawrence's alter ego Paul Morel in the autobiographical *Sons and Lovers*, we hear that "He was not strong enough for heavy manual work": D. H. Lawrence, *Sons and Lovers* (London: Penguin, 2006), chapter 5. Hereafter cited as "*Sons*."

15. The full statement reads: "There is, however, the third thing, which is neither sacrifice nor fight to the death: when each seeks only the true relatedness to the other. Each must be true to himself, herself, his own manhood, her own womanhood, and let the relationship work out of itself. This means courage above all things." D. H. Lawrence, "Morality and the Novel," in *Study of Thomas Hardy and Other Essays*, 174–5.

16. *D. H. Lawrence: The Critical Heritage*, ed. R. P. Draper (London: Routledge, 1997), 71. Hereafter cited as "Draper."

17. Benjamin Kunkel makes the same point in an article in the *New Yorker*, 19 December 2005: "People talking about Lawrence sound like his own quarrelsome couples: they hate him, they say, or they love him, or both."

18. John Middleton Murry, *Son of Woman* (London: Cape, 1931), 173.

19. *The Letters of D. H. Lawrence*, Vol. V, ed. J. Boulton and L. Vasey (Cambridge University Press, 1989), 201.

20. D. H. Lawrence, *Women in Love* (London: Penguin, 1982), 430. Hereafter cited as "*Women*."

21. See in particular M. Ragussis, *The Subterfuge of Art: Language and the Romantic Tradition* (Baltimore: Johns Hopkins University Press, 1978), and M. Bell, *D. H. Lawrence, Language and Being* (Cambridge University Press, 1992).

22. D. H. Lawrence, *Studies in Classic American Literature* (Cambridge University Press, 2003), 14.

7

Worthy Writers, Worthy Readers

> Piecing together the history of these families, I have often come
> across people who have been dispossessed, defrauded or disowned,
> as often happens with illegitimate births or children abandoned
> by their parents. There are often members of the family who
> end up in a mental hospital, prison or other institution because
> they are considered, rightly or wrongly, unworthy to be a part of
> the community in which they should belong.
>
> Valeria Ugazio, *Permitted and Forbidden Stories*, 229.

With Dickens we move into an entirely different atmosphere and
world of meaning than that which prevails in the authors we have
considered so far. Fear and courage are present of course; an awareness of success and failure is very strong and stronger still an awareness of good and evil. But dominating all of these considerations is the
question of belonging. One is or is not accepted in a family, a community, be it school or law courts or club or commercial company. One is
or is not happy with the other members of the community and with
one's own being defined by belonging to it. Rather than gathering
steam towards some particular trial, or focusing on the development
of a particular character, Dickens's stories follow a number of characters, placing them in and out of this or that group in a game where
exclusion can be accompanied by intense pathos if the character concerned is one the reader sympathizes with, or again vindication and
even triumph if the character is perceived as an evil intruder. But
inclusion in a family or group can also cause anxiety if the person
included feels the others in the group are not worthy of him or her. In
this case the family is a prison, not a home. In general what determines a person's right to be part of the group is not simply their goodness or badness, but their *worthiness* of the group; or we could say that

goodness is understood as a quality *functional to the group* and badness as a quality *destructive of the group*. In general the novels are full of figures whose relation to the family they live in is complex, arduous: an adopted niece, a friend's widow, the prospective spouse of a deceased child. Other family members declare their character in the way they deal with these figures whose right to belong is not absolutely established by hereditary right, but depends on their generosity.

Two key events in Dickens's life inevitably colour any discussion of his representation of family, poverty, and Victorian endeavour. The first we all know about from school days since it constitutes *the* Dickens legend: his having been sent out as an 11-year-old boy to work in a factory while his father was in a debtors' prison. The desire to have this traumatic experience authenticate Dickens's adult concern for the urban poor and explain his later depiction of any number of child waifs (one critic has counted 318 orphans in Dickens's fiction) tends to obscure the real nature of the young Charles's suffering as he later and very emotionally recalled it for his friend and biographer, John Forster (but never for members of his close family). He was not beaten, starved, or ill-treated. The factory was run by an acquired cousin, son of a widower who had married Charles's aunt. Charles worked there for a year or a little less before returning to school and normal middle-class life.

What intensely upset the young Dickens was that he was the only member of the family to be sent off to earn his keep in demeaning circumstances. His elder sister Fanny continued to study at the Royal Academy of Music where the fees were 38 guineas a year (at the factory Charles was earnings six shillings a week). Apparently the girl had a bright, honourable future while he did not. His younger siblings lived together with their mother and father in Marshalsea Prison, which was not, thus, quite the place we imagine when we think of a Victorian prison. For Charles, alone in cheap lodgings, "utterly neglected,"[1] the experience was one of seemingly punitive exclusion from the family circle and what he begged for initially was not to be spared the factory, but to be lodged nearer Marshalsea so as to be able to share his meals with his parents. There was also the shame, as this ambitious middle-class child saw it, of being obliged to consort with "common men and boys" (Forster, 29) and worst of all of being seen amongst them by friends of the family who occasionally came to the factory shop. Charles was meant for better things and better company. In general, the working class, in Dickens's writings, are an underworld into which a boy from a better family can unjustly be thrust.

If one is singled out for exclusion, it is not unreasonable to fear that there might be grounds for this, that one might indeed be unworthy in some way, or again that simply by being excluded one might *become* unworthy, become tainted at least in the eyes of one's peers. In this regard Victorian mores could not be more different from ours today, where to have poor origins, or to have lived for a period in poverty, is more a boast than a stigma. Dickens later referred to himself at this time as "a small Cain," though he had "never done harm to anyone" (Forster, 28). The sphere of exclusion, experienced as privation, is supposed normally to be in relation to the moral sphere, a punishment, but in his case punishment was unjust.

One can well imagine that a response to this traumatic experience might be to seek to demonstrate one's worthiness at all costs in order to regain a secure position inside the domestic circle and the community at large. In fact Dickens would spend much of his life putting himself at the head of a numerous family, in control of magazines that were home to many writers and illustrators, read by a large number of families, and in general at the heart of English society and a wide community of readers whom he would soon be referring to as "my family."

The second unhappy event stands in direct relation to the first, though this is rarely pointed out. Those who write enthusiastically about Dickens, and he does inspire warmth and enthusiasm, never seem to regret that he had to work in a factory as a boy, since there is a consensus that without this experience he might not have become the novelist we admire; but the same people do very much regret that thirty-four years later Dickens excluded his wife (and mother of his ten children) from the family, not only separating from her, but keeping the family home and custody of the children for himself (the youngest was only 6 at the time) and frowning on every contact between them and her. In *Charles Dickens, A Life*, Claire Tomalin remarks: "The spectacle of a man famous for his goodness and attachment to domestic virtues suddenly losing his moral compass is dismaying," to the point, Tomalin tells us, that, "You want to avert your eyes…" (p. 293).

So again, together with an act of exclusion—one member of the family cast into outer darkness—comes the question of blame and worthiness. In letters to his friend Forster, Dickens had admitted he was not without blame for the deterioration of his marriage, but when he actually forced the separation he put all the blame on his wife, accusing Catherine, in private and in public, of not being fit for her role, of laziness and lassitude, "weakness and jealousy," of "not caring" for the children, whom she "was glad to be rid of."[2] She was not worthy of him or them. Catherine is even accused of not having the spirit to fight for her place in the family. Her defeatist acceptance of banishment is confirmation of her unworthiness.

The uneasiness of biographers in the face of this marital breakdown suggests how contagious when reading Dickens is the habit of taking sides over matters of inclusion and exclusion. His narratives draw us into his own way of thinking about the world to the point that biographers feel obliged to let us know their personal sentiments of disappointment and dismay. So the whole fraught question of belonging and not belonging, of being worthy or unworthy, inside a respectable group around the merry fire (with Little Em'ly or Tiny Tim) or outside in the damp darkness (like Oliver Twist or Little Nell, or again Little Em'ly after her fall), also colours the reader's response to the writer himself. Reading biographies of Dickens we feel we have been invited into his happy family, only to be disappointed with the man who brought it into being. But then disappointment was Dickens's own defining and constant experience with his family; great expectations coming to nothing. "I never sing their praises," he remarked of his children, "because they have so often disappointed me."[3]

Dickens married Catherine Hogarth in 1836 when he was 24 and she 20. He had only recently got over an earlier love for a well-to-do girl whose family rejected him because he was young and without good career prospects. Another exclusion. Eldest of nine children, Catherine was better placed socially than Dickens; her father was an editor on a newspaper that Dickens was writing for. Marrying her, Dickens was gaining entry to more respectable society. The move was not entirely distinguishable from his urgent project to become part of the literary world and be loved and accepted by England's readers. Serialization of *The Pickwick Papers* was under way, inviting everyone to become involved in the droll Pickwick Club. In 1837 the book's success won Dickens election to the more real Garrick Club.

The marriage took place on 2 April and the first child was born on the following 6 January. Nine months almost to the day. From then on the Twelfth Night of Christmas would always be an occasion of rumbustious family celebrations and elaborate theatricals of which Dickens was both creator and main performer. Over the next fifteen years nine other children would follow, plus miscarriages. So although Dickens would increasingly show unease about the numbers of his children, at one point claiming he'd only ever wanted three and even regretting he'd ever had any at all, there was a wilfulness in this rhythm of production, again not entirely distinct from the enormous effort of will that must have been involved in writing *Pickwick* and *Oliver Twist* simultaneously, then beginning *Nicholas Nickleby* nine months before *Oliver Twist* was finished, obliged to meet deadline after deadline in order to respect monthly serialization schedules. By the time the tenth and last child was born Dickens was publishing his ninth novel. It was 1852 and he was 40. He was also editing a magazine, *Household Words*, had briefly edited a newspaper, published highly popular Christmas stories every festive season, as well as scores of essays and articles throughout the year, *and* ran a home to rehabilitate fallen women; they were all activities that put him at the centre of other people's attentions and (great) expectations. His children vied constantly for his affection, his readers eagerly awaited their monthly fix from his pen, other writers sought inclusion in his magazine, destitute women presented themselves for admission to his home. He was involved in society in every possible way, by far the most popular author in the land. He *belonged*. No one could exclude him, though there was always the possibility that he might isolate himself, as someone now too worthy and too remarkable to demean himself with the group, or immerse himself in it for too long, setting out on long walks and trips alone, as his alter ego David Copperfield often does in moments of depression when society seems to offer only disappointment. A year after his admission to the Garrick Club, Dickens resigned from it. In each of the following three decades he would rejoin the Garrick and resign again in protest over this or that issue, moving dramatically in and out of the community it offered. Belonging wasn't what he had hoped it would be.

The sense of ambitious expectation is plain enough in the names of the Dickens children. Charles chose the names. Catherine was given no say in the matter. The first was Charles Culliford Boz Dickens. Charles after himself, of course, and Boz too, since that was the pen-name he had used for his early work. Culliford was the second name of Charles's maternal uncle, Thomas Barrow, a cultured man who had forbidden Dickens's father ever again to come into his house after the latter failed to honour a loan of £200. An exclusion. Dickens identified with this more respectable side of the family and often visited the house from which his dishonourable father was banished.

The second child, a girl born in 1838, was named not after Catherine, but after her younger sister Mary who had died some months before. The child's second name, Angela, reflected the fact that Dickens had always and rather extravagantly considered Mary "an angel." Here one has to pause to mention that Dickens never lived and only rarely spent time with his wife alone. From the beginning he had invited the 17-year-old Mary to live with them and after she died another younger sister, Georgina, was brought in to take her place.

Even at moments when one might have expected exclusiveness and intimacy—wedding anniversaries, for example—Dickens generally invited a third to the party, for preference his close friend Forster. It was conviviality rather than intimacy that interested him, a conviviality in which Dickens, flamboyantly dressed in lavishly coloured silks and velvets (dress is a powerful index of worthiness in his novels), invariably played the role of animator and entertainer. It is curious when we look at his narratives, how many of his famous characters are actually double acts; in *David Copperfield* there are the Murdstones, brother and sister, Steerforth and his mother, the Micawbers, man and wife, Uriah Heep and his mother, Aunt Trotwood and Mr Dick, Dora and her friend Julia, Agnes and her father; but David himself, like other Dickensian alter egos, is never quite locked into any relationship. In general there is very little man/woman intimacy in his fiction. It is as if the most natural meeting Dickens can imagine is that of himself, alone, in the presence of at least two others, who draw him in, or repel him.

After Charles Culliford Boz and Mary Angela the next child, Catherine Macready, took her mother's name followed by that of a leading male actor, William Macready, a close friend of Dickens's. From this point on the names grow ever grander: Walter Landor (after the poet and friend), Francis Jeffrey (after the founder of the *Edinburgh Review* and friend), Alfred D'Orsay Tennyson (after both the French artist and dandy and the English poet, both friends), Sydney Smith Haldimand (after the famous wit and the philanthropist, both friends), Henry Fielding ("in a kind of homage," Forster had been told, "to the style of the novel he was about to write": Forster, 523). An exception is the ninth child, Dora Annie, named after the brainless girl David Copperfield loves and whom Dickens, at the very moment of the child's birth, had just decided to kill off, as it were, in print, thus giving his hero an easy way out of his inappropriate marriage. In the event, baby Dora also died, only months after her fictional namesake. The last boy was Edward Bulwer Lytton, named after the aristocrat and hugely popular novelist, who, needless to say, was a friend of Dickens and who was published in Dickens's *Household Words*.

With the one exception of Dora, then (a tribute to his own genius perhaps, since he felt that Dora was one of his best characters), Dickens was creating a thick web of worthy belonging for his family, placing them at the heart of contemporary cultural life, and making them constantly aware of the ideal of artistic achievement. Along with the official names, however, Dickens also gave his children nicknames, often more than one, usually in cartoon contrast to the grandeur of the baptismal name. So Charles, who soon became Charley, to distinguish him, but also diminish him, was also Flaster Floby, or the "Snodgering Blee." Mary was Mamie or Mild Glo'ster. Catherine was Katey, but also the Lucifer Box. Walter was "Young Skull." Francis was Frank, but also Chickenstalker (after a comic character in Dickens's story "The Chimes"). Alfred was Skittles. Sydney was Ocean Spectre, or just Spectre. Henry was the Jolly Postboy and the Comic Countryman. Edward, having been extravagantly announced in Twelfth Night home theatricals, aged 3, as Mr Plornishmaroontigoonter, became Plornish and then simply Plorn for all his life, to the point that he was hardly referred to by his baptismal name at all.

In Dickens's fiction, giving nicknames is an indication of one character's hold over others, for good or ill. In *David Copperfield* David's peremptory Aunt Betsey insists on calling him Trotwood (her own surname), then just Trot, as a condition of his being accepted into her household; Dora she calls Little Blossom. David allows the sinister

Steerforth to call him Daisy, a name that immediately asserts the inequality and ambiguity of their relationship.

No sooner was Charley born than Dickens was sending lavish descriptions of the boy in letters to friends, a practice that would be repeated with each successive birth. Dickens had learned in adolescence that exaggerated imitation was always popular; it was thus that he had won the admiration of his fellow clerks when he worked in law firms in his teens and it is thus that David Copperfield establishes a place for himself among his companions at Mr Creakle's school. Dickens was a talented mimic and saw how people were always excited to recognize another's foibles. He had developed this talent in written form in his *Sketches by Boz* and again in *Pickwick* where a happy complicity between reader and writer is fostered through relishing caricatures from a world both share. Now, the author's children too were rapidly transformed into comic sketches to amuse his friends and impress upon them the Dickens family's domestic happiness. The continuity between the world of the novels and the letters describing the children is remarkable. Nicknames to the fore, tales were told of the children's prodigious abilities and infant achievements, their father present throughout as boisterous master of ceremonies. The thrust of almost any act of writing by Dickens was to conjure the world through imitation, compelling the admiration of the reader and creating a sense of shared, celebratory belonging. In short, the writing was a powerful extension of his behaviour with friends and family.

It is fascinating how enthusiastic biographers become in recounting this festive and extravagantly documented aspect of Dickens's fatherhood, as if they had a personal investment in his exuberance. This is the cheerful mood that reading Dickens instils. "He was a magical father," David Gottlieb tells us, "loving, generous and involved. He romped with [his children], took them on long walks, sometimes exhausting them with his preternatural energy...He had a special voice for each of them. How could they not adore him?" (Gottlieb, 236) The same might be asked of the reader of Dickens, who often experiences his fiction as a wonderfully exuberant act of generosity, calling into life for us a dramatis personae of charming eccentrics. "A national benefit," enthused Thackeray of "A Christmas Carol," "and to every man and woman who reads it a personal kindness."[4] Nobody would ever say words like this of any writing by Hardy, Lawrence, or Joyce. It is rather as if Dickens had become a literary Father Christmas, and we were his happy children forever unwrapping bulky presents.

Inevitably, Charley was the first to appreciate that the jolly situation might be difficult to grow out of. As a child, you could prove yourself a worthy member of the Dickens household simply by satisfying your father's rigid rules regarding room-cleaning, bed-making, general tidiness, and strict punctuality (Dickens personally inspected his children's bedrooms every morning, exacting punishment if anything was out of place); but as one got older it all became rather confusing, and here we begin to see the darker side of this mind set.

From the age of 12 to 15, Charley was sent to Eton, hence introduced to the heart of the English upper classes, but despite doing well there Dickens withdrew him. The upper classes were not his people. He didn't want a son with a sense of "entitlement," but a worker and fighter like himself; Charley must be "pampered in nothing" (Gottlieb, 37). Entitlement was the opposite of worthiness, the one conferred by birth, the other earned by endeavour. Dickens in fact had begun to marvel that his children were not as determined and hard working as he was. Charley had "less fixed purpose and energy than I could have supposed possible in my son." Indeed "he inherits from his mother . . . an indescribable lassitude of character" (Gottlieb, 37). It does not seem to have occurred to him that a certain passivity on the part of wife and children might be a natural response to his own energetic monopoly of the domestic stage, to the point of ordering the family groceries himself and insisting on the exact arrangement of the furniture. "For twenty years," writes Gottlieb, without quite seeing the sad comedy of the situation, "[Dickens] exhausted himself trying to strengthen [his children's] willpower and forward their careers" (Gottlieb, 38).

But how much like himself did Dickens really want his children to be? Great mimic as he was, he frequently referred to himself as "the Inimitable One." Charley had composed a play at 8 and shown some talent for translating and writing, but Dickens decided that his future was in business and sent him off to Germany to learn German, which he supposed was the business language of the future. After some modest success as a bank employee, and a far from shameful failure in business deals with China, Charley would eventually be allowed to become Dickens's assistant in *All The Year Round*, the magazine that replaced *Household Words*. Later it would be the second son, Walter

Landor, who enjoyed writing but was discouraged from continuing. It must be confusing to be named after a poet yet told not to write. Walter's older sister Katey, who took her second name from a great actor, would later be forbidden by her father from taking up a career in acting. These activities risked imitation of The Inimitable One.

In his celebrated essay on Dickens, a strange combination of admiration and perplexity, George Orwell complains that the author's characters have "no objective except to marry the heroine, settle down, live solvently and be kind..." after which "everything is safe, soft, peaceful and above all domestic...the children prattle round your feet...there is the endless succession of enormous meals, the cold punch and sherry negus, the feather beds and warming-pans...but nothing ever happens except the yearly childbirth. The curious thing is that it is a genuinely happy picture, or so Dickens is able to make it appear."[5]

Dickens was indeed able to make it appear like that, at least in the early years, but in putting his finger on this aspect of his novels, Orwell was also signalling a genuine problem in Dickens's life. The happy family, or his place at the heart of the happy family, was the be all and end all, but Dickens hadn't reckoned with the children growing up, the childbirths coming to an end, and his depressive, often sick wife proving less than a constantly cheerful and admiring companion. Disappointed, his assessments of family and children began to oscillate alarmingly as he switched between the roles of exuberantly performing father, delighted with his adoring offspring, and depressive, self-excluding, long-range walker disgusted with a tribe of hangers on. "You don't know what it is," he wrote of his sons to one friend, "to look round the table and see reflected from every seat at it (where they sit) some horribly well-remembered expression of inadaptability to everything" (Gottlieb, 17). Of Walter, he remarked "I don't at all know this day how he comes to be mine or I his" (Gottlieb, 84).

At a loss with his children, or indeed with a character in his books (Micawber, Little Em'ly), Dickens sent them as far away as possible. He had tried this with his embarrassing parents, renting them a house in Devon, a form of exclusion without infamy. Thus the would-be writer Walter was prepared for an army life in India, leaving for the subcontinent, never to return, aged 16; all the younger boys were sent away to a cheap, gloomy boarding school in Boulogne, whence they came home (to be entertained by their father) only once, or occasionally twice, a year. Eventually, Francis Jeffrey (Frank) departed for India aged 19, Alfred for Australia aged 20, Sydney joined the navy and sailed on a first three-year mission aged 14, Plorn, the saddest and shyest of the troupe, sailed for Australia never to see his parents again, aged 16. There was an element of denial in all this, a pretence that the old sense of belonging had not been betrayed; simply a parent or child was removed from one's presence so that the disappointment that came from being associated with him or her was relieved. Only the eighth child, Henry, managed to convince his father he was worthy of bearing the Dickens name in London and got himself sent to Cambridge University and trained in the law at great expense.

Expense was now a key issue, since the children who left England, or whom Dickens had sent away—Walter, Frank, Alfred, Sydney, and Plorn—all ran up debts. Walter borrowed heavily in India, writing home frequently to ask for money; Alfred liked the same kind of fancy clothes his father wore; in the navy Sydney spent heavily in every port, giving his father's famous name as security. At this point, Dickens had no real financial problems but complained bitterly and eventually cut off both Walter and Sydney, forbidding the latter to return home and even remarking of him, in a letter to his brother Alfred, that "I begin to wish he were honestly dead" (Gottlieb, 104). Again it did not occur to Dickens that using one's wealthy father's name to run into debt was a way of insisting on kinship from a distance, as if to say "you can't get rid of us so easily." In all his novels, money and the way it is used, with meanness or benevolence, is crucial to the construction of relationships and a sense of belonging, Scrooge being the most obvious and celebrated example.

Marvelling at the "vitality" that Dickens invests in the happy family as an end in itself, Orwell, writing in 1940, concludes that this is an indication of the hundred years that have elapsed since the novelist was working, with the implication that society has now moved on and our energies are directed to more interesting and urgent questions than happy families. It's worth noting here that when a writer who perplexes us in some way comes from a different time we can always reassure ourselves that his mind set is so odd because of the intervening years and social changes. In fact, of course, there were many writers of the mid nineteenth century who did not share Dickens's investment in happy families at all.

Turning back to Ugazio's book on semantic polarities, her chapter on depression includes examples of many families who still make the issue of belonging, of inclusion or exclusion, the critical criterion of value in their lives. In particular she looks at members of such families who find themselves oscillating "between two equally unacceptable alternatives" (Ugazio, 234): they feel they have to belong to the family or stay in a particular relationship, because they can see no place for themselves in the world outside it, but at the same time they are convinced that the relationship dishonours them and that family and friends are unworthy of them. Such subjects frequently regard their spouses as "inadequate by nature," so that "preserving the relationship contributes towards making them feel unworthy and excluding them from what they feel to be their rightful destiny" (p. 240). "It is a most miserable thing to feel ashamed of home," Pip tells us in *Great Expectations*.[6]

Let's now consider *David Copperfield* with an awareness of this pattern of behaviour, remembering that it was written in 1849 and 1850. At this point Dickens, at 37, was reaching the height of his fame with seven novels written and seven children born. 1847, however, had marked the onset of his wife's migraines and general depression, conditions that would intensify over the coming years, while 1848 would see the last of Dickens's series of Christmas stories, those moments where family festivity and literary endeavour are most happily and successfully brought together.

Even before the narrative begins, the preface, or prefaces, establish the special world of emotion we enter when we read Dickens. This is from the first preface:

> I do not find it easy to get sufficiently far away from this Book, in the first sensations of having finished it, to refer to it with the composure which this formal heading would seem to require. My interest in it, is so recent and strong; and my mind is so divided between pleasure and regret—pleasure in the achievement of a long design, regret in the separation from many companions—that I am in danger of wearying the reader whom I love, with personal confidences, and private emotions.[7]

Companions, separations, a relationship of love with the reader...In the second preface, years later, he remarks of the first,

> So true are these avowals at the present day, that I can now only take the reader into one confidence more. Of all my books, I like this the best. It will be easily believed that I am a fond parent to every child of my fancy, and that no one can ever love that family as dearly as I love them. But, like many fond parents, I have in my heart of hearts a favourite child. And his name is DAVID COPPERFIELD.

All children are children, but some will be at the centre and some at the periphery. All relationships are thought about as family relationships.

As the story opens, young David, Dickens's beloved (because Dickens's alter ego), grows up with his kind, weak mother; the child is orphaned before birth of his father, who lies, excluded by death, in the graveyard close to their house.

> There is something strange to me, even now, in the reflection that he never saw me; and something stranger yet in the shadowy remembrance that I have of my first childish associations with his white grave-stone in the churchyard, and of the indefinable compassion I used to feel for it lying out alone there in the dark night, when our little parlour was warm and bright with fire and candle, and the doors of our house were—almost cruelly, it seemed to me sometimes—bolted and locked against it. (*David*, chapter 1)

It is immediately established that to be outside the warm home is, in a real sense, to be dead. The mood is set. Let me say, in parenthesis, that none of our other authors could have written these lines. One speaks a great deal of the power of the imagination, but it is always the imagination of a particular person with a particular background and position. Thomas Hardy simply would not have thought this. If anything he would have envied the dead in their graves, beyond fear and desire and responsibility. Equally, Dickens could not have imagined Sergeant Troy's sword display and Bathsheba's reaction. It was not his territory. These reflections are not inconsequential. In a sense they offer the most telling rebuttal of those who raise the "biographical fallacy" objection to any comment on an author's life.

At David's birth his Aunt Trotwood arrives to take over or threaten the family. The intruder, comic, violent, or sinister, is a common figure in Dickens's work, for there is no happy family unit without someone to threaten its happiness. To a point it is the threat that makes us aware of the happiness and the happiness is constructed against the threat. In this case, however, the Aunt proves innocuous. Her life ruined by a bad marriage, she loathes men and will only get involved in David's family if the child born to her dead brother is a girl. Seeing David is a boy, she flees.

David's mother is the focus of his affection, but weak, malleable. These failings make her inadequate to protect the boy. She is lovable but in the end not worthy, not able to construct and defend a home. She thus allows herself to be duped by the second, this time terrifying intruder, Murdstone, who, supported by his even more atrocious sister, hides his opportunism behind a façade of puritan and utilitarian rigidity. Together brother and sister, who see life in terms of winning and losing, but hide this semantic between interminable talk of good and evil, will conspire to exclude David from the family and have him sent to Mr Creakle's school.

Meantime, however, the faithful nurse servant, Peggotty, has introduced David to her own family, a kind of refuge as his disintegrates. As always in Dickens, much attention is given to the house in which the family lives. Here we have a powerful contrast between desolate nature and warm hearth: "There was a black barge...high and dry on the ground [its] chimney smoking very cosily...It was beautifully clean inside, and as tidy as possible....After tea, when the door was shut and all was made snug (the nights being cold and misty now), it seemed to me the most delicious retreat that the imagination of man could conceive" (chapter 3).

The description of the Peggotty family at once establishes the fantastic fertility of Dickens's imagination and its restricted territory; the issues are always the same, but within it he can think of endless permutations. Old Mr Peggotty has at different times adopted a nephew and a niece from different branches of the family, as well as offering hospitality to Mrs Gummidge, widow of his dead partner, but no

one must ever mention this benevolence of his that holds the rather
precarious family together:

> The only subject…on which he ever showed a violent temper
> or swore an oath, was this generosity of his; and if it were ever
> referred to, by any one of them, he struck the table a heavy blow
> with his right hand (had split it on one such occasion), and swore
> a dreadful oath that he would be "Gormed" if he didn't cut and
> run for good, if it was ever mentioned again. (chapter 3)

"Gormed" is Mr Peggotty's private word. Language is crucial in
establishing community and each community that Dickens describes
has certain words to use which is to declare one's belonging ("umble,"
for example, is the key word in the family/conspiracy that is Heep
and his mother). In this case "gormed," a word no one actually
understands, establishes the fierce taboo surrounding the act of generosity that founded this particular family. Needless to say, Dickens's
mastery of all the languages of all the families and communities he
describes establishes his belonging to all of them and by extension
the reader's.

Paradoxically, Mrs Gummidge constantly underlines the happiness
of the Peggotty family by complaining that she is "a lone lorn creetur"
(chapter 3) when clearly she is not. She has the constant company of
the others. Cheerfulness is a duty in Dickens and to moan is to be
unworthy. Inevitably, David responds by wishing to exclude her.

> I was very sorry for her; but there were moments when it would
> have been more agreeable, I thought, if Mrs. Gummidge had
> had a convenient apartment of her own to retire to, and had
> stopped there until her spirits revived. (chapter 3)

Later in the novel, when the family is struck by disaster and her help
is required, Mrs Gummidge is miraculously transformed:

> What a change in Mrs. Gummidge in a little time! She was
> another woman. She was so devoted, she had such a quick per-
> ception of what it would be well to say, and what it would be
> well to leave unsaid; she was so forgetful of herself, and so
> regardful of the sorrow about her, that I held her in a sort of
> veneration. (chapter 32)

Mrs Gummidge shifts from one extreme to the other of the semantic in which all the characters are involved. In the same way a Hardy character like Eustacia Vye can shift from rash to fearful, bold to ter-rified, or a Dostoevsky character from great sinner to great saint. It is often in the smaller, almost caricature figures and their dramatic oscil-lations that the critical polarity is at its most naked.

David makes his own contribution to the Peggotty community dur-ing his visit by reading aloud to them and to Little Em'ly in particular. It's a gesture that shows his generosity, but also underlines the fact that despite his attraction to their home and in particular to Little Em'ly, David can never become part of this family, for he comes from another class and has quite other aspirations. However wonderful in herself, Little Em'ly would not be worthy of him. Later, when the Murdstones take over his own home and David is banished to his room in punish-ment for having bitten Mr Murdstone's hand, he seeks belonging in the virtual community of novel characters:

> From that blessed little room, Roderick Random, Peregrine Pickle, Humphrey Clinker, Tom Jones, the Vicar of Wakefield, Don Quixote, Gil Blas, and Robinson Crusoe, came out, a glo-rious host, to keep me company…This was my only and my constant comfort. When I think of it, the picture always rises in my mind, of a summer evening, the boys at play in the church-yard, and I sitting on my bed, reading as if for life. (chapter 4)

Dickens gives us here a fairly clear statement of the function of liter-ature as he experiences it. To offer community. (Virginia Woolf has very much the same vision.) The author's constant winks at his own readers, with asides and observations on David's part that he could not possibly have made at that age, establishes a complicity between Dickens and his own readers (whom he loves) exactly in line with this idea. Writer and reader are at one in their observation of the story. However, just as David is superior to the Peggotty family whom he reads to, so Dickens is benevolently superior to the community of readers he writes for.

Exiled to Mr Creakle's school, David's strategy for getting himself accepted by the other boys shows all the dangers of needing too urgently to belong. He shares food with the others, he tells them sto-ries, he offers comic imitations. In particular, he seeks an alliance with the popular Steerforth, imagining him a worthy leader of the boys, when beneath the charming surface he will prove cynical and unreliable. It is David's eagerness to belong that makes him blind, a common failing in Dickens's alter egos; Pip will make the same mistake again and again in *Great Expectations*.

The novel's pattern is now well established: throughout we see David moving from one group or family to the next, constantly seeking to establish what is his position and whether others are truly worthy members or not, whether they accept him or not, meantime experiencing and causing the reader to experience the full gamut of emotions attached to this way of seeing the world. Mr Creakle's school, for example, exhibits all the negative behaviour that in Dickens's vision is the opposite of benevolence and cheerfulness. It is dystopia to the Peggotty utopia. Creakle is mean, grumpy, cruel to the point of sadism, with hints of paedophilia:

> I should think there never can have been a man who enjoyed his profession more than Mr. Creakle did. He had a delight in cutting at the boys, which was like the satisfaction of a craving appetite. I am confident that he couldn't resist a chubby boy, especially; that there was a fascination in such a subject, which made him restless in his mind, until he had scored and marked him for the day. I was chubby myself, and ought to know.
> (chapter 7)

Yet Mr Creakle's school is as nothing to the factory that David is banished to after his mother's death, even though here there is no cruelty. At the school David could at least make friends with other boys of the same class. In the factory friendship is unthinkable, because these boys are beyond the pale, infinitely beneath him. Dickens's "family" does not extend to the whole nation, only to the worthily literate. We have here one of the first examples of our hero falling into depression from a sense that those around him are not worthy of his company:

> No words can express the secret agony of my soul as I sunk into this companionship; compared these henceforth everyday associates with those of my happier childhood...and felt my hopes of growing up to be a learned and distinguished man, crushed in my bosom. The deep remembrance of the sense I had, of

being utterly without hope now; of the shame I felt in my position; of the misery it was to my young heart to believe that day by day what I had learned, and thought, and delighted in, and raised my fancy and my emulation up by, would pass away from me, little by little, never to be brought back any more; cannot be written. (chapter 11)

Words create community, but are inadequate to express the agonies of exclusion from it, or inclusion in a community that is beneath our dignity. Words, communication, are in a sense only possible where there is shared belonging. Again:

That I suffered in secret, and that I suffered exquisitely, no one ever knew but I. How much I suffered, it is, as I have said already, utterly beyond my power to tell. (chapter 11)

Where before cheerfulness and friendliness were virtues, in this underworld self isolation is the only possible course:

I never, happily for me no doubt, made a single acquaintance, or spoke to any of the many boys whom I saw daily.... I led the same secretly unhappy life; but I led it in the same lonely, self-reliant manner. (chapter 11)

Working at the factory, David is lodged with the Micawbers, who, Dickens later explained, were based on his parents. Remarkable here is the conflict between genuine affection for this family unit and repugnance for the endless pretensions and fraudulent manoeuvring of Micawber himself, who oscillates in no time at all between fantasies of supreme worthiness and moments of intense depression and abasement, a grotesque, accelerated caricature of David's more subtle swings of mood. At the end of the book, of course, the unworthy but lovable Micawbers will be dispatched to Australia.

One could go on forever quoting from *David Copperfield* showing how even the tiniest encounter invariably fits into the pattern, often in the most bizarre ways. Fleeing the factory in desperation David seeks out his long lost aunt (the search for lost family members is a constant Dickens trope), who is always on anxious watch for donkeys, or indeed pedestrians, intruding on her lawn. Again we have the sense of the family under threat, and, as always in Dickens, comedy alternating with misery. Aunt Trotwood generously includes David in her house-hold, sees off Murdstone and his sister in grand style (they must never cross her lawn again!), and pays for her nephew's education at Doctor Strong's school, allowing him to lodge with the Wickfield family, hon-ourable people who share his class and aspirations, but whose weak-nesses (like David's mother's) make them vulnerable to another home-wrecker and social climber, the dreadful Uriah Heep, a man who constantly plays the card of his supposed humility, his endlessly repeated recognition of his own unworthiness, in order to become a member of the class he nevertheless dishonestly aspires to. Notably, attempting to fit in at Doctor Strong's school, David is now afraid of appearing to know about things that a middle-class boy should not know about:

> troubled as I was, by my want of boyish skill, and of book-learning too, I was made infinitely more uncomfortable by the con-sideration, that, in what I did know, I was much farther removed from my companions than in what I did not....How would it affect them, who were so innocent of London life, and London streets, to discover how knowing I was (and was ashamed to be) in some of the meanest phases of both? (chapter 16)

David's concern offers a sense of why Dickens himself was silent for so long about his own childhood vicissitudes. Both character and author seem to accept as reasonable the community's concern about someone with this kind of knowledge. So in showing knowledge of these things in his book was Dickens himself risking suspicion? It would seem not, since nobody did suspect, except of course Forster, who had already been told. One of the advantages of novel-writing, then, for Dickens is that one can give expression to a range of experi-ence without suffering the consequences that would be inevitable if the same experience were openly confessed. That said, Dickens would later seem to have decided that this might not be true of all "danger-ous" knowledge, since he never gave us an alter ego who has a mistress in secret, something that was his own—one imagines intense—experience in the last ten years of his life. In this particular regard he was careful to observe all the proprieties.

Thanks to hard work and talent, David does well at school, shines first at the law courts, then as a writer, taking his rightful place in society and justifying all those who believed in him, but makes the mistake of marrying Dora, who, despite her higher social class, is not intellectually or spiritually or temperamentally worthy of him. David now falls into a conflicted state; he has invested everything in the idea of domestic bliss, and indeed in convincing Dora's father that he is worthy of her social class, but is increasingly frustrated that Dora is holding him back. As in the factory, though in a very different way, he is living beside someone who demeans and belittles him, though this time it is his fault, or the fault of blind love, of inexperience, or simply of his compulsive determination to seduce and belong. Sadly, but actually fortunately—and one sees here Dickens's difficulty taking on this dilemma in a serious way—Dora dies (childless, of course) and in her dying words actually explains the truth to David, and, perhaps outside the story, to Catherine:

> But, as years went on, my dear boy would have wearied of his child-wife. She would have been less and less a companion for him. He would have been more and more sensible of what was wanting in his home. She wouldn't have improved. It is better as it is. (chapter 53)

The wife here is allowed a dignity in having internalized, accepted, and corroborated her husband's criticism of her. One could, with a little generosity, feel the pathos of Dora's personal growth in adversity, her willingness to open to her husband on something that he knows but has always denied. Alternatively you could say this was hardly Dickens at his most attractive.

Like all Dickens's fiction, *David Copperfield* seeks to be generously inclusive of a wide range of language habits and accents, as if drawing readers in to one vital and bustling, but always middle-class society. The range of reference is wide, but never, as in other writers we have looked at, abstruse; that is, the reader, particularly the reader of the time, never finds the text too difficult, never feels excluded by the author's erudition. Dickens presents himself as brilliant, affable, but never forbidding or distant. The whole tone and strategy is of inclusion, at least towards those who read and have the price of a magazine. At the same time, and it is precisely this that consolidates the identity of the community Dickens is forming, he always makes clear which villainous members (Heep, Steerforth, Murdstone) should be excluded from our society, if possible killed off or imprisoned. There is absolutely no ambiguity here. If there is a grey area, an area of regret we might say, it is with those we loved who fell by the wayside, those who weren't morally strong enough, who let the side down, without being actively evil. After Little Em'ly makes the catastrophic mistake of running off with Steerforth, she isolates herself from the family, goes into voluntary exile, accepting her unworthiness and prompting her old uncle to search for her as far away as Italy. One need only compare Dickens's treatment of Em'ly with Hardy's of Tess to appreciate that while the society being talked about is essentially the same, the world of values and emotions these writers live in is utterly different. Hardy doggedly denies that Tess has done anything wrong, depicting society as blind in its condemnation of her, blind as bad weather, or mere bad luck. Dickens on the other hand accepts entirely that, however charming, Em'ly has indeed done something wrong and must be punished. Interestingly, Dickens never suggests that it is unkind of Em'ly, after having fled, not to let her family know if she is alive or not; the sin is so great that it is understandable that she imagine they want nothing more to do with her. Old Mr Peggotty's willingness to search for her is the exception, not the rule, and even after she is found there is no question of her living a respectable life in England. She will have to join the Micawbers on the long trip to reincarnation in Australia.

There is a conflict here, a difficulty establishing where one really stands over a crucial question at the heart of the values around which meaning is constructed; how is it possible that the author's vision of community allows no way of mending a mistake born of passion, short, that is, of having the good luck to have one's badly chosen partner die? How is it possible that Dickens, who already begins to feel that he is in a marriage that is not what he wanted, cannot really write about such things?

After Dora's death David withdraws from the world of his youth to spend some months of intense depression abroad. Here Dickens is unconcerned about displaying a knowledge of depression that seems to go far beyond the requirements of the story, becoming almost an essay on the gamut of emotions (in particular those of desolation and unworthiness) to which the author himself was periodically subject.

From the accumulated sadness into which I fell, I had at length no hope of ever issuing again. I roamed from place to place, carrying my burden with me everywhere. I felt its whole weight now; and I drooped beneath it, and I said in my heart that it could never be lightened.

When this despondency was at its worst, I believed that I should die. Sometimes, I thought that I would like to die at home; and actually turned back on my road, that I might get there soon. At other times, I passed on farther away,—from city to city, seeking I know not what, and trying to leave I know not what behind. (chapter 58)

When his mind starts to turn to Agnes as a possible partner, his immediate reaction is a sense of unworthiness. David cannot look to Agnes for salvation from his unhappiness, since he himself has behaved unworthily (in *Great Expectations* Pip has the same feelings about Biddy); the only way to recover honour now is *not* to return to her, but to have the strength to be alone.

I had always felt my weakness, in comparison with her constancy and fortitude; and now I felt it more and more. Whatever I might have been to her, or she to me, if I had been more worthy of her long ago, I was not now, and she was not. The time was past. I had let it go by, and had deservedly lost her. (chapter 58)

In the event, David does return to Agnes and eventually overcomes his feelings of unworthiness to propose marriage. There is no mention of any sexual attraction. The novel then closes with a round-up of all the families and relationships it has presented, projecting them into the future, putting each person in the place he or she deserves.

From the publication of *David Copperfield* onward it was all downhill as far as Dickens's domestic life and peace of mind was concerned. Disappointed with wife and children, Dickens had begun to flirt with younger women. The edifice of success so determinedly constructed, of family, friends, and readers, was becoming a straitjacket.

The situation might seem analogous to Hardy's, but Dickens had a vastly greater investment in family and indeed in the whole question of honour connected to occupying a leading role in a family. Also, while Hardy's need to be courageous pushes him towards the self exposure he fears, Dickens has no such impulses. He is neither concerned with convincing himself he is courageous, nor does he allow himself to be governed by fear. He deals aggressively with publishers. He is rarely apologetic. He throws himself into the fray of social politics, he accepts tough assignments without concern, he joins clubs and leaves them, confident in his decisions, makes friends and abandons friends, sure in his choices. Responsibility is no problem. But honour is. To lose his honour is to lose his identity. And his honour is wrapped up in his role as family man.

As the situation at home precipitates, his fiction undergoes a transformation that reaches a near pathological peak in the extraordinary *Little Dorrit*, written and published in the years immediately before the break-up. Orwell complains in his essay that while Dickens's characters are intensely and immediately striking, the melodramas they are involved in are muddled and forgettable, "crossword puzzles of coincidences, intrigues, murders, disguises, buried wills, long lost brothers" (Orwell, 83). In the early novels the focus on a single child and his or her biography creates a simple story that takes the reader through. This disappears later on; the plotting grows more complex and apparently capricious, fragmenting into a succession of intensely described psychodramas often held together with the most bizarre links in a world where almost everything is not quite what it seems and almost everyone defending a secret that might destroy their reputation. For Orwell these plots constitute an "enigmatic episode"; he cannot see what they are about. Yet with an eye on the semantic of belonging and Dickens's increasingly unstable position in it, the apparent muddle is soon all too clear.

Little Dorrit is too vast to summarize, but here are a few core details. The widowed Mr Dorrit is in Marshalsea Prison as a result of defaulting on debts contracted with he knows not whom. His life paralysed for years (a frequent trope in Dickens) by this pre-Kafkaesque situation, he has become "the Father" of the prison, sees the prisoners and guards as his extended family, and struggles in every way to maintain the dignity of his immediate family. Later he inherits a fortune he knew nothing of and is released from gaol into wealth.

So although obsessed with control Mr Dorrit has none at all over the main events of his life; every major development is entirely mysterious to him. Behind the mystery lies the vast and evil bureau-cracy of the Circumlocution Office, a government ministry that does everything to make the lives of the country's citizens unliveable. Arthur Clennam, one of the novel's main centres of interest, a man seeking to uncover some secret regarding his birth that his estranged mother refuses to reveal, is attracted to Mr Dorrit's daughter, Amy (Little Dorrit), who sometimes works for his mother. Clennam tries to help Mr Dorrit and another man by appealing to the Circumlocution Office, but partly as a result of this he himself ends up in Marshalsea Prison. The whole novel is saturated in prison imagery, with frequent superimposition of the ideas of prison and family.

Freed and wealthy, Mr Dorrit takes his family to Italy where he eventually decides to marry the governess he has employed for his children, the pompous, tedious, unattractive, but doubtless *respectable* Mrs General. He seems to be doing this more from lack of imagination than any real desire, as if society demanded it of him. If anything, he has a more intimate relationship with daughter Amy than with the governess, she being the one triumphantly good person in the novel, embodying all the qualities on the positive side of the belonging semantic: generosity, compassion, diligence, etc. It was Amy who looked after her father in prison and upheld the dignity of the family. Mr Dorrit is jealous when his innocuous brother Frederick spends time with Amy, and the night before proposing to Mrs General he comes out with this "Freudian" slip: "You have not kissed me, Amy. Good night, my dear! We must marry—ha—we must marry YOU, now." It appears that the person Mr Dorrit yearns for is his daughter, or a woman like his daughter.

Needless to say, Mr Dorrit is concerned to prevent anyone's knowing the shameful secret of his years in prison, but it is precisely as he tries to do the boring, respectable thing, proposing to Mrs General in view of once again establishing a conventional family, that the world breaks up around him and he begins to imagine that, rather than an Italian palazzo, he is back in prison in the Marshalsea. Eventually, at a dinner party, he breaks down completely, acting as though he were in the prison and repeatedly calling out the name of his favourite gaoler, at which point the shameful secret of his prison life is revealed. Abandoned now by everyone but Amy and his brother

Frederick, in the space of a few days Mr Dorrit simply declines and dies. Frederick, who has been a loyal, lifetime companion, can't accept the separation:

> The only utterance with which he indulged his sorrow, was the frequent exclamation that his brother was gone, alone; that they had been together in the outset of their lives, that they had fallen into misfortune together, that they had kept together through their many years of poverty, that they had remained together to that day; and that his brother was gone alone, alone! (chapter 19)

This is the semantic of belonging at its most plaintive. Soon afterwards, Frederick himself also passes away, kneeling over his brother's corpse. But if her father and uncle are both killed by this loss of family honour, Amy's initial reaction to his disgrace is that "She was not ashamed of it or ashamed of him." Dickens thus creates a situation where the fact of social disgrace is confirmed, there is no life for a Mr Dorrit after it, but the main focus of sympathy in the book does not accept this, though she does not fight it either. Dickens's position seems entirely conflicted here, which perhaps explains the book's extraordinary emotional intensity. Later, after interminable vicissitudes, Clennam, who is twice Amy's age (and thus not perhaps so far from Mr Dorrit's), is allowed to marry her, but only after all his family have died. Free from any "old belonging," anyone who might make him feel ashamed, he can start a new life, in poverty, with the much younger Amy, the thing her father also seemed to want to do.

I hope that the idea I'm working towards is clear. Dickens, in desperate crisis in his own marriage at this point—and one cannot exaggerate how huge this problem must have seemed to a man who had built his whole self image and career on the idea of family harmony—uses his novel to explore emotions of entrapment, disgrace, responsibility, and above all the question, is it ever possible to be free from one's past? Without telling "his own story" or any story remotely like his own, he nevertheless creates episodes whose emotional unity is precisely this sense of an insuperable conundrum at the heart of life, a secret, or many secrets, that distort the language of the characters in all kinds of evasiveness, some of it bordering on the pathological.

In 1855 Dickens had eagerly arranged an appointment with Maria Beadnell, his fiancée of more than twenty years ago, writing her excitedly romantic letters, only to flee disappointed when he discovered what she had become—an overlarge, rather dull lady. In 1857 he completed *Little Dorrit*. The same year he met the young actress Ellen Ternan, who was to be his companion for the rest of his life. In 1858 he ordered his wife to leave the family home and separation proceedings began.

Initially, Dickens seems to have hoped he might simply present himself as in the right and continue in the old way without any loss of reputation or self esteem. He had been right to expel her, he claimed, because she was unworthy: "She does not—and she never did—care for the children: and the children do not and they never did—care for her" (*Letters*, vol. 8, 632). He wrote to the papers and told them so. People were not convinced. Dickens was now unusually out of tune with friends, family, and readers. The philanthropist, Miss Coutts, withdrew her financial support for his home for fallen women. His son Charley disobeyed him and went to live with his mother. Dickens then voted against Charley's inclusion in the Garrick and refused to go to his wedding.

On the professional side, having argued with the publishers of the magazine he edited, *Household Words*, Dickens was now starting a new magazine and decided he would call it *Household Harmony*. As if nothing had happened! Friends intervened to change his mind. With his wife now expelled from the family home, he proposed to rent the house to the Ternan family—Ellen, her sisters, and her mother. Again friends convinced him this would be unwise, it would suggest he had a liaison with Ellen. Dickens hesitated, then backed down.

With the long performance of the happy family now over—"The so happy and yet so unhappy existence which seeks its realities in unrealities, and finds its dangerous comfort in a perpetual escape from the disappointment of heart around it" (*Letters*, vol.7, 354)—the author's life split into two parts. Theatricals with his children were substituted with dramatic readings to a much larger family of public audiences all over Britain and the USA. The first British tour, shortly after the separation, took in an astonishing eighty-five towns. Rather than simply reading from his work, Dickens adapted and rewrote passages to offer elaborate and exhausting dramatic performances often running to two hours. Although he spoke of his need for money, and the readings were extremely profitable, on another level this emotional engagement with adoring audiences clearly satisfied a need to consolidate his place at the heart of society, even though the books he was writing suggested more and more that the society he was seeking to impress did not impress him.

Supporting Ellen's mother and two sisters financially while denying loans to his sons in far-flung empire, Dickens hurried back and forth between his readings, his official home with his wife's sister Georgina in Rochester, and the various places—Paris, London, Slough—where at different times he hid Ellen. He had forbidden her to go on with her acting (an unworthy profession for a woman) so that inevitably she was entirely dependent on him. His constant restless travelling over the next decade, immensely complex arrangements with false names and mysterious methods of payment to maintain Ellen in secret, suggests the impossibility of his ever reconciling the impulses pulling his life apart. He needed Ellen, but his honourable position at the centre of society was central to his identity.

Needless to say these conflicting impulses and the consequent impasse fed the fiction over these years. *A Tale of Two Cities* (1859) again features a man, Dr Manette, unjustly imprisoned and unable to shake off his past. Again betrayals inside families, pretences, disguises, and even unwillingness to recognize family members are frequent. Inspired by the—odd idea—of someone who "retires to an old lonely house...resolved to shut out the world and hold no communion with it" (Schlicke, 259), *Great Expectations* sees Dickens return to the first person for a deeply pessimistic re-run of the *David Copperfield*-style *Bildungsroman*. Again the hero, Pip, is a peripheral member of a family, working class this time, and immediately he is pulled in two directions: downward, not into a factory, but into the confidence of a convict; and upward into the noble house of Miss Havisham, trapped in the past of her old and disappointed betrothal. As soon as he has met Miss Havisham and her ward Estella, yet another child in the guardianship of someone other than her parents, Pip is in agony over his humble background, desperate to belong to this more dignified, as he supposes, society. Throughout the book he finds himself rejected by the upper-class world he wishes to belong to and deeply ashamed of those he does belong to. The emotion reaches a climax when he discovers that the income he depends on for living like "a gentle-man" in fact comes from the convict, Magwitch, who has made the secret donation more as part of a personal and self-regarding fan-tasy than from any serious reflection on Pip's well-being. He simply wanted to make his own personal gentleman. "I am afraid the dreadful truth," Pip tells his friend Herbert, "is that he is attached to me, strongly attached to me. Was there ever such a fate?" (*Expecta-tions*, 41) He belongs where belonging is demeaning. Though the situation is utterly, one might say oneirically transformed, the emotion is exactly that which Dickens frequently expressed when talking about his wife and children. And in both cases "respectability" depends on this attachment to someone who is felt to be the wrong person. To "leave" Magwitch, for Pip, is to lose the very basis for his being a gentleman.

As with *Little Dorrit*, *Great Expectations* breaks all the links between money, class, and worthiness, an equation which, at least ideally, had held in the earlier books. Estella herself will turn out to be Magwitch's child, hence not the person Pip thought. Corroding all the assump-tions on which polite society was based, Dickens seems to be looking for a position where the only thing that matters is the inner qualities of a person, the positive and beneficial nature of a relationship. If he can convince himself of this perhaps he can shake off his chains and come out in the open with Ellen. But again and again in *Great Expecta-tions*, one feels that despite all the rhetoric his alter ego Pip remains anchored to his prejudices and impulses, the conventional view being internalized to the point where it is impossible to break out of it. Speaking of "the singular kind of quarrel with myself that I was always carrying on" (chapter 27), he admits that despite his realizing that Estella is not worthy of his affections, nevertheless he can't "avoid that wonderful inconsistency into which the best and the wisest of men fall every day" (chapter 27).

The same year as he began publishing *Great Expectations*, Dickens burned his private papers and letters, ordering his youngest sons to bring baskets and baskets of papers out to a bonfire in the garden. Whether this was done, as in Hardy's case, for fear of what posterity might have discovered, or more in an attempt to free himself from the past, isn't clear. Dickens made much in his readings of alternat-ing between cruel and kind characters, monsters and saints, even remarking that he felt he was all the characters in his novels, the cruel as well as the kind. In his readings he seemed to take special pleasure in performing the cruellest characters, as if, like the Iatmul Indians in Bateson's *Naven*, he found relief in being allowed to exhibit a side of his character that the Victorian proprieties obliged him to deny. Here, in the opening pages of the author's last complete novel, *Our Mutual Friend*, is a guest at one of the Veneerings' *nouveau-riche* dinner parties describing Mr Harmon, the father of the novel's protagonist, and a man who has made his fortune in rubbish collection, a dustman:

> The moral being—I believe that's the right expression—of this exemplary person, derived its highest gratification from anathematizing his nearest relations and turning them out of doors. Having begun (as was natural) by rendering these attentions to the wife of his bosom, he next found himself at leisure to bestow a similar recognition on the claims of his daughter. He chose a husband for her, entirely to his own satisfaction and not in the least to hers...[8]

This was sailing terribly close to the wind. Dickens too had thrown out his wife. Dickens too had objected to various of his children's marriages. Soon we hear that Harmon's father sent Harmon to a cheap school in Brussels, as Dickens had sent his sons to a cheap school in Boulogne. It is extraordinary how much energy Dickens invests and how much pleasure he takes in presenting a grotesque version of himself. One begins to understand that his writing had perhaps always allowed Dickens to occupy both extremes of the semantic polarity in which all meaning in his work is constructed. Unable to find a stable position in the real world, one can be a whole dramatis personae on the page, creating exactly that famous literary "ambiguity" that critics routinely so admire.

Eventually the effort of trying to be both respectable father of a vast family of readers and a lover with intimate domestic needs pushed Dickens to exhaustion. Needing to be at the centre of attention himself, he was sharing his life with a woman who must never be seen at all. Each reading tour ended with new physical ailments and acute depression. "I am nearly used up..." he wrote to Forster (*Letters*, vol. 12, 86). And to another friend, "I am here, there, everywhere and (principally) nowhere" (*Letters*, vol. 11, 348), a telling statement on his position, or lack of it, in the world of belonging.

Did literature help Dickens in any way to resolve his problems, or did the popularity it gave him actually make this more difficult for him? The question is not idle speculation, given the general desire to see literature as positive and necessary. On one level, as we have seen, his writing allowed him to identify with various different positions with regard to the complex question of belonging. On the other, in life away from the page he came to be identified so powerfully with the respectable family man that it was difficult for him to move away from that position.

But if literature failed to help Dickens, or helped him only in one way and trapped him more deeply in dilemma in another, does and can it "help" the reader? Again, if this seems an inappropriate question, let me insist that one cannot subscribe to the general pieties about literature without asking it. Isn't it precisely the obsession with worthiness and honour that saturates his writing that makes it impossible in the end for Dickens to resolve the problem with Ellen? And won't that obsession, communicated to the reader, have the same crippling effect? Ellen herself, it seems, felt unworthy of Dickens, felt she was endangering his career. She entirely shared his values. Did he deny the relationship so determinedly, one wonders, to the point of breaking off his friendship with Thackeray, for example, because he felt at some level ashamed of her?

A subplot in *Our Mutual Friend* has the lawyer Eugene Wrayburn eventually marrying the boatman's daughter Lizzie Hexam. Despite being in love with Wrayburn, Lizzie, like Ellen, is loath to ruin his reputation by associating with him and it is only after she saves his life when he is assaulted and left for dead in the river, then personally nurses him back to health, that he can marry her, with the excuse that now that she has been so closely associated with him marriage is necessary *to save her reputation*. This is wishful thinking. The novel closes with another dinner party at the Veneerings' home where this controversial marriage across the class divide is discussed; Dickens fields all the respectable folks' response to it, no doubt imagining what reaction might be to his own eventual open association with Ellen. "The question before the committee," one of the party begins the discussion with complacent irony, is, whether a young man of very fair family, good appearance, and some talent, makes a fool or a wise man of himself in marrying a female waterman, turned factory girl.

All those present find the marriage grotesque and utterly unacceptable, until, last of all, the mild-mannered Mr Twemlow is questioned:

"I am disposed to think," says he, "that this is a question of the feelings of a gentleman."

"A gentleman can have no feelings who contracts such a marriage," flushes Podsnap.

"Pardon me, sir," says Twemlow, rather less mildly than usual, "I don't agree with you. If this gentleman's feelings of gratitude, of respect, of admiration, and affection, induced him (as I presume they did) to marry this lady—"

"This lady!" echoes Podsnap.

"Sir," returns Twemlow, with his wristbands bristling a little, "YOU repeat the word; I repeat the word. This lady. What else would you call her, if the gentleman were present?"

This being something in the nature of a poser for Podsnap, he merely waves it away with a speechless wave.

"I say," resumes Twemlow, "if such feelings on the part of this gentleman, induced this gentleman to marry this lady, I think he is the greater gentleman for the action, and makes her the greater lady. I beg to say, that when I use the word, gentleman, I use it in the sense in which the degree may be attained by any man. The feelings of a gentleman I hold sacred, and I confess I am not comfortable when they are made the subject of sport or general discussion."

"I should like to know," sneers Podsnap, "whether your noble relation would be of your opinion."

"Mr Podsnap," retorts Twemlow, "permit me. He might be, or he might not be. I cannot say. But, I could not allow even him to dictate to me on a point of great delicacy, on which I feel very strongly." (chapter 17)

With this last remark we arrive at the heart of the problem: the extent to which one's own opinion is to be dictated by the opinion of others, above all one's "noble relations." Twemlow is admired here for his independence, his ability to construe a notion of honour and worthiness that runs counter to the run of received opinion. But if Dickens was able to imagine a future open relationship with Ellen thus, he never acted on his feelings, rather accepted a divided life and worked himself into the ground until the inevitable collapse and early death in 1870, aged 58.

Notes

1. John Forster, *The Life of Charles Dickens* (Chicago: University of Michigan, 2008), 26. Hereafter cited as "Forster."

2. *The Pilgrim Edition of the Letters of Charles Dickens*, 12 vols, ed. Kathleen Tillotson, Graham Storey, and others (Oxford University Press, 1965–2002), vol. 8, 632. Hereafter cited as "*Letters.*"

3. Robert Gottlieb, *Great Expectations, The Sons and Daughters of Charles Dickens* (New York: Farrar, Straus and Giroux, 2012), 17. Hereafter cited as "Gottlieb."

4. In *The Oxford Companion to Charles Dickens*, ed. Paul Schlicke (Oxford University Press, 1999), 468. Hereafter cited as "Schlicke."

5. George Orwell, *A Collection of Essays* (New York: Harvest, 1981), 87. Hereafter cited as "Orwell."

6. Charles Dickens, *Great Expectations* (Harmondsworth: Penguin, 1999), chapter 14. Hereafter cited as "*Expectations.*"

7. Charles Dickens, *David Copperfield* (Harmondsworth: Penguin, 2004), Preface to the 1850 edition. Hereafter cited as "*David.*"

8. Charles Dickens, *Our Mutual Friend* (Harmondsworth: Penguin, 1998), chapter 2. Hereafter cited as "*Friend.*"

Conclusion

We Must Defend Ourselves

If reader reactions to writers are profoundly conditioned by their respective backgrounds, by where the one is writing from and the other reading from, then any notion of establishing a definitive "judgement" on a book, or pecking order of writers, is swept away. But it could hardly be otherwise, and despite all the literary prizes and "authoritative" critics, really we already knew this. "He didn't get it at all," "she bought into it at once" are expressions that suggest how readily we accept the idea of affinity or lack of it when we read a book; publishers and newspapers send novels to reviewers who they sense will be well-disposed to a certain style or content; relatives and friends give gifts of books they hope will be the right thing for the right person. Often the person receiving the book appreciates at once that a mistake has been made. It's an experience I'm all too familiar with.

So this is common knowledge. If anything, the interesting thing here is how little is written about these matters, how completely excluded they are from literary criticism or even the book pages of the newspapers. On the contrary, critics, particularly academics, fiercely argue their own positions. I cannot offhand think of a single critic who regularly separates out the question of writerly ability from the impact of the book on people with different values systems, different life visions.

Why is this? Why is no science applied to a phenomenon we have all observed, as if personal taste were to be left for ever a mystery? Perhaps because no one is eager to deconstruct or schematize his or her own responses, to relativize his or her own position. Perhaps we have to pretend that individual background is not important in order to allow a debate to take place at all, otherwise we would always be turning back to the question of why we think as we do. More likely each of us dreams in the end that our own position might prevail, might prove "right": we want there to be a best writer, a finest achievement, and we want it to be the writer and book that was most important for us. Similarly the writer himself wants to believe that his book can impress everyone; he doesn't want to think that so and so likes his novel mainly because of the way it intersects with his own experience.

This brings us to the status of authors and of literature. Here I have proposed a model for narrative creativity that is *not* common knowledge and that has uncomfortable implications. It is widely believed that literary writing may come out of mental turbulence, disturbance, even pathological states of mind. Yet it is always assumed that the literature produced by these states of mind is beneficent. Why should this be? Is it perhaps that since we enjoy reading narrative it has become important for us to believe that the activity is intrinsically good; we exploit a cod Platonism absorbed since earliest infancy that tells us that if a thing can be described as beautiful it will somehow be morally good as well. A great thinker like Schopenhauer was convinced that novels were detrimental to mental and moral health. People were "deluded into an absolutely false view of life by reading novels."[1] Nobody takes on this accusation. Schopenhauer is a great thinker, except when inconvenient.

I have tried to give some shape and system to our intuition of the mental discomfort behind much literary creativity. I have not questioned whether Dickens, Hardy, Lawrence, Joyce, etc. write "good" novels or stories. All these writers are triumphantly seductive. What I wonder is whether the process of fiction writing offers resolution, greater ease, to the writer or the reader, or whether it is a way of rendering an unhappy situation chronic, by allowing just sufficient consolation and reward from the expression of unhappiness to prevent us from making big changes. True, I have suggested, in my very title, that writing can be thought of as a survival skill, offering relief from internal conflict, but perhaps in some cases we could add, *in lieu of some other more radical and practical course of action*: if you are not willing, that is, to undertake the real life changes that might resolve a dilemma, or if such changes have been tried but proved impossible, unworkable, then write!

In this regard I recall a conversation with a German writer, locked into an unhappily complicated relationship with two women and writing rather brilliant books about men locked into unhappily complicated relationships with more than one woman. He was fairly young and over beers complained to me that he found himself doing things (with women) that he had promised himself he would not do, repeating "mistakes" (with women) that he had promised himself he would not repeat. However, when I suggested he might want to see an analyst, he responded that he was afraid that if he solved his problems it would affect his writing. Perhaps he needed this messy life to write. Literature, or an income from literature, or the self esteem that accrues from producing literature, were more important than solving his unhappiness, or made unhappiness manageable.

The strategy rubs off on the reader. When we read Colm Tóibín's silvery prose, the fine cadences with which emotional suffering is described, it really does seem that art might somehow make up for, or *almost* make up for, a lost love, an empty life. Alice Munro is on the same wavelength: successful writing, sophisticated reading, sensibility, irony, deep perception, all invite us to feel at once pleasantly sad, yet complacent about lives described as failures. The reader of Hardy can feel gratified by his or her own rejection of destructive Victorian values, yet at the same time remain convinced of how dangerous it is to go against the social grain. And so on. Perhaps of all writers, Beckett, or at least his narrators in the trilogy, made most hay with this, at once mocking the consolation to be found from writing—"There's a choice of images," declares Malone, having described his alter ego's disorientation as a "thistledown plucked by the wind"—then finding consolation in this superior awareness that no consolation is to be had.

Let me return to Bateson's *Naven* to frame the one deep question I meant this book to pose. Bateson described a drastically imbalanced society which found in an elaborate and bizarre series of rituals a way of allowing that imbalance to continue without the society tearing itself apart. Whether this is precious stability or chronic unease is not an issue for the anthropologist, but it might well be for the individual members of that society. It might be that, becoming conscious of the mechanism, an individual of that society would want to drop the ritual and confront the imbalance. In general, then, is the effect of the novels we read essentially a form of *Naven*, an elaborate mental ritual? Thus the virtual and virtuous intellectual life is sufficiently gratifying, one way and another, to permit us to continue with ugly realities; the satisfaction of feeling ourselves progressive, for example, is enough to allow us to go on being conservative. Arguing against arousing compassion in novels, Muriel Spark remarked that the sentiment merely allows readers to "feel that their moral responsibilities are sufficiently fulfilled by the emotions they have been induced to feel."

Is this the way our western lifestyle perpetuates itself? With a structural hypocrisy that requires a very special mind set; receiving the Nobel Prize, the winner gives a ferociously anti-capitalist speech to a full-house of international capitalists who all applaud warmly. Nothing will change. Such was the case when José Saramago took the award. "I can't understand why they applauded," remarks The Writer in Bernhard's play *Am Ziel*, speaking about his own successful drama: "we are talking about a work that exposes every one of them and in the meanest way admittedly with humour, but nasty humour, if not with malice, true malice. And all of a sudden they applaud!"[2] Art has become structural to our way of life, not a force for change, rather an opportunity to feel complacent about our sensibilities.

Not that I believe that all literature is necessarily of this kind. Of the writers we have looked at Lawrence is definitely of a different nature. Beckett is another writer determined to draw attention to the dangerous consolations of literature, to satirize the power of art to encourage us to imagine our sufferings noble.

But on the whole? Amid all the pieties that art is always worthy and above all worthy of funding, that the world needs stories, regardless of what kind of stories, let us stay focused on the real effect that reading and writing has on us. Let us understand the malaise it came out of and the malaise we bring to it. Plato banished poets from his republic. He felt they were noxious. Plato was not a fool. I will not suggest we do the same, I love reading novels; but let us beware, or rather be aware. Dickens can be harmful. Hardy can be harmful. Joyce can be harmful. I admire them all. We must defend ourselves.

Notes

1. Arthur Schopenhauer, *Essays of Schopenhauer* (Auckland: The Floating Press, 2010), 75.
2. In Gitta Honegger, *Thomas Bernhard* (New Haven: Yale University Press, 2001), 36.

Index